WIZARDS
THAT PEEP

WIZARDS THAT PEEP

A JOURNEY INTO THE OCCULT

Siegbert W. Becker

NORTHWESTERN PUBLISHING HOUSE

Milwaukee, Wisconsin

Second edition, 2010

Northwestern Publishing House
1250 N. 113th St., Milwaukee, WI 53226-3284
© 1978 by Northwestern Publishing House
Published 1978
Printed in the United States of America
ISBN 978-0-8100-0054-4

23 24 25 26 27 28   11 10 9 8 7 6

Contents

Editor's Note vii

Introduction ix

1 Divination or "Fortune-Telling" 1

2 Magic and Witchcraft 28

3 Spiritism 56

4 Demonic Possession 78

5 Satanism 103

Scriptural Index 123

EDITOR'S NOTE

Our present generation's obsession with the occult is painfully obvious. Witches and warlocks, Satanists and astrologers have boldly intruded upon the American scene — not to mention the spate of movies on the occult plus current T.V. offerings! A generation ago this would have been most unlikely. But the "occult explosion" has happened, and Bible believing Christians are asking questions: Is there such a thing as devil possession today? What really happens at an exorcism? Is there something sinister about the Ouija board? How about water dowsing? How can you explain the impressive predictions of some fortune tellers? Didn't some of Luther's staunch friends cast horoscopes? And so on and on.

In his usual clear, incisive style, Dr. Siegbert Becker of the Wisconsin Lutheran Seminary, Mequon, Wisconsin, addresses himself in the present volume to the complex subject of occultism. A popular essayist and preacher, Dr. Becker minces no words in "telling it like it is." But even the most sensational subject matter is soberly judged by the inerrant Word. "Our best defense against the modern explosion of the occult," concludes Dr. Becker, "is not more knowledge of the occult on our part . . . the best weapon is the Gospel of God's redeeming love in Christ who has come to destroy all the works of the devil . . . " Pastors will find some welcome counsel in the concluding remarks titled "The Christian Pastor and the Occult." We think you will agree WIZARDS THAT PEEP is a modest little volume of abiding relevance and contemporary significance.

Loren Schaller

Introduction

The past decade has seen a veritable explosion of interest in the occult and a remarkable change in attitude toward the occult. The scientific research in the field of parapsychology made popular by J. B. Rhine at Duke University and now being carried on in many scientific laboratories has helped to prepare the way for the acceptance of many occult phenomena and has made interest in the subject academically respectable, at least in all but the most anti supernaturalistic circles. The repeal of the laws against witchcraft in England a quarter of a century ago has also encouraged many practitioners of the occult to admit openly to what was once generally considered to be deviant behavior.

The amount of literature being produced in the area is stupendous and the varieties of occult phenomena is surprising, at least to those of us who can still remember what the attitude of society toward the occult was only about a generation ago. In 1948 Rudolf Bultmann could write, "Now that the forces and laws of nature have been discovered, we can no longer believe in spirits, whether good or bad."[1] When the French scholar Jules Michelet in the middle of the nineteenth century wrote what at least one edition of the *Encyclopedia Britannica* is reported to have called "the most important work on medieval superstition yet written,"[2] he could treat witchcraft as a crime invented by the church as an excuse for burning poor women who tried in the only way they knew how to find some alleviation of the miseries to which the feudal society and the church of the Middle Ages subjected them and their families. And even in 1961 the Spanish scholar Julio Caro Baroja could still write, "A world which accepts magic is, above all, a world that accepts slander."[3]

Before we begin the consideration of the various types of occultism it might be well for us to consider the options that are open to men when they come face to face with these phenomena. It is possible, of course, to write the whole business off as fraud and trickery from beginning to end. The other extreme is to consider all occult events as perfectly normal happenings which are not understood as such because we have not yet discovered the laws of nature that underlie them and that they could, therefore, be duplicated by anyone who is a partner to the secret involved. Between these two extremes lies the view that some occult occurrences are real but paranormal, and therefore limited in their performance to those who have special gifts. These gifts are still considered to be part of the natural world. Another possible view is that occult phenomena, at times at least, are truly supernatural events that can come to pass only by the intervention of spirit powers.

While it is possible that any one of the four views may apply to a specific case, yet the one option that is not open to a Bible-believing Christian is the conviction that all occult phenomena must be cases of fraud and deception. At the very least he will have to grant that there have been real cases of devil possession, at least in the days of Jesus' visible sojourn here on earth. A Christian can not, therefore, accept the absolute impossibility of occult events in principle as is done by the materialistic philosophy which has dominated our modern world for so long. There are clear indications in the Bible that the forces of the spirit world may be able to have a far more direct influence on human behavior and concrete physical events than we often suppose possible.

In this connection I sometimes wonder whether Gausewitz's translation of the second commandment was not influenced by the opinion that occult occurrences are impossible, at least at the present time. Gausewitz says, in his translation of Luther's *Small Catechism* that we should not misuse God's name by practicing superstition. This is his translation of Luther's word "*zaubern*." The word superstition, at least in modern American usage, implies a belief that has no connection with objective reality. When Luther used the word "*zaubern*" he certainly had reference to the use of magic and sorcery, about the reality of which he seems to have had no doubt. Gausewitz's translation of Luther's words, however, seems to imply that all occult phenomena lack objective reality and are the product of trickery and overactive imagination. But very likely a generation ago few people expected to have to deal with actual cases of witchcraft in twentieth century enlightened America.

Today, however, we must once more deal with the problem, and Luther's words telling us not to profane God's name by using witchcraft are very much in place. It is not our business to determine whether instances of occult involvement are real or fraudulent deception. Actually, aside from the kind of divine, inerrant revelation we have in the Bible, it is probably impossible to decide with certainty the question of whether we are dealing with evil spiritual powers that have intruded into our physical world or with a clever trickster. Or could it be both? The story of the Fall certainly demonstrates that the devil can do things which many 20th century scientists would call impossible and that the devil can use truths for his fraudulent ends.

It is enough for us to know that all involvement with the occult is a violation of God's holy Law. It may, however, occasionally be of some value for us to be acquainted with the various forms of occult involvement so that we may recognize the enemy when we meet him. Moreover, we must be careful to distinguish the truly occult from what we do not understand. Certain cases of telepathy and clairvoyance, for example, may be purely natural occurrences.

When the various aspects of the subject are studied, one is often reminded of the fact that the occult is the devil's mimicry of the mighty works of God or, as Luther says, that the devil is God's ape. God sends His prophets into the world to guide men on the way to heaven; and the devil sends his messengers to lead men astray by divination. God empowers Moses to do miracles in order to persuade the people to believe God's Word; and the devil apparently empowers the magicians of Pharaoh to help harden the king of Egypt in his unbelief. God inspires holy men to speak His Word; and evil spirits from hell speak through trance mediums. The Holy Spirit comes to live in our hearts and to move us to lead sanctified lives; and the devil takes possession of the souls of men to lead them to blaspheme God and spit out obscenities. God seeks our worship and asks us to honor Him in our lives; and the devil seeks that worship and honor for himself and gets it from the proponents of Satanism in our time.

These are also the five areas into which we have chosen to divide our discussion of the subject of the occult.

1

Divination or "Fortune-Telling"

"Let now the astrologers, the stargazers, the monthly prognosticators, stand up, and save thee from these things that shall come upon thee. Behold, they shall be as stubble; the fire shall burn them; they shall not deliver themselves from the power of the flame."

Isa. 47:13,14.

Divination, which is derived from the Latin word *divinare*, to foresee or foretell, is the art of discovering without the use of the five normal senses information about secret things that are far removed from us in time or space. Just where one is to draw the line between what is called extrasensory perception and divination is sometimes very difficult to establish. There are people who question whether such a line should be drawn at all, but it would seem that there are instances of mental telepathy and clairvoyance that are perfectly natural, even if they might be called paranormal, and others which must be denounced as the kind of divination which is clearly forbidden in Scripture.

Unbelieving scholars have the habit of classifying the activity of the prophets with heathen divination. To them Samuel's words about the asses of Kish (1 Sam. 9:1-20) are on the same level with the revelations of a gypsy fortune-teller. The visions of Daniel, if they are not pure invention, are no different qualitatively from those produced by the clairvoyance of Jeane Dixon. But the Bible makes clear that there is a difference. The one is forbidden while the other is viewed as a gracious gift of the Lord, and even the magicians of Pharaoh had to admit that the power behind the miracles of Moses is the finger of God (Exod. 8:19). The devil is

1

truly God's ape, as Luther says, but we know from the infallible Scripture that the difference between true prophecy and false divination is as great as that between heaven and hell.

THE POSSIBILITY OF DIVINATION

The rationalistic theology which has for so many years dominated the thinking of large segments of the visible church and the materialistic philosophy which lies at the root of many of the pronouncements of science in our time generally question even the existence of a spiritual world outside of and beyond this visible material universe of which we are aware through our five senses. Even when the existence of spirits is not denied, it is often seriously questioned whether there can be any physical or mental contact between the spiritual and material worlds. Any predictions concerning the future would have to be based on past experience and on scientific knowledge of the laws of nature or of human psychology. Any prediction that has its origin in the spiritual world and which comes supernaturally to men either from God and the angels or from evil spirits is *a priori* excluded from the realm of possibility.

It is, however, with such supernaturally derived predictions, either real or pretended, with which we deal when we speak of divination or fortune-telling.

A Bible-believing Christian, who takes the Scriptures at face value, will not deny that supernatural prediction of future events is possible. The Bible contains many such prophecies. It should be noted that in the Bible the word "prophesy" does not always mean to foretell the future. A prophet, in Biblical terms, is one who speaks for someone else. When Moses insisted that he was not a capable speaker, God sent Aaron with Moses to be his "prophet," that is, to speak for Moses (Exod. 7:1). Men served as God's prophets when they said of past, present, or future events what God wanted them to say.

The Bible contains many predictions of future events. The prophets not only foretold the coming of the Messiah, together with many details concerning His work, His birth, and His death, but they also predicted many specific events that transpired in the history of God's people in the Old Testament. Micaiah, for example, foretold the defeat of Ahab and Jehoshaphat by the Syrians in the battle at Ramoth-Gilead (1 Kings 22:1-28). Elisha, dur-

2

ing a period of hopeless famine, predicted that the price of bread would drop dramatically within twenty-four hours (2 Kings 7:1). Many other such examples could be cited.

The Bible also makes clear that the knowledge of the future that the prophets had came to them in a supernatural way from God. As an example we may point to the book of Revelation, in which the apostle John says that he will write of things that "must shortly come to pass," but he also states that this revelation came to him from God (Rev. 1:1). When Joseph was asked to interpret the dreams of Pharaoh he disclaimed all ability to do such a thing by his own natural powers. He told the king of Egypt that the interpretation of his dreams would have to come from God (Gen. 41:16). In the same way Daniel, in interpreting the dream of Nebuchadnezzar, said that it was God who was revealing the secrets involved in the dream of the Babylonian king (Dan. 2:28). It might be noted here that this story demonstrates rather clearly that God in some mysterious way established direct contact both with the mind of an unbelieving heathen and with that of His inspired prophet (Dan. 2:28). The possibility of direct revelation from God in a supernatural way is so clearly and definitely taught in Scripture that no Bible-believing Christian can deny that the foretelling of the future is possible.

As has already been indicated, such revelations from God do not necessarily deal only with the future. According to Scripture it is possible to gain supernatural knowledge of events which happened in the past or which are happening in the present in faraway places with which no natural contact exists. Thus Samuel could tell Saul that the donkeys for which he was looking were back home (1 Sam. 9:20). And if we accept the first chapters of the Bible as a correct report of creation, this already implies that God must have, in some miraculous way, revealed everything that happened at least up to and including the creation of Adam, for up to that moment there was no human observer from whom that report could have come. Man simply cannot have any scientific or empirical knowledge of creation. There is, therefore, a good reason why also the historical books of the Old Testament were called "prophetic books" by the Jews. Even in their recording of past events, the holy writers were acting as spokesmen for God, and in writing the accounts of the past they were also guided by the inspiring Spirit of God. While much of what they wrote about the past could be obtained from human sources, yet some things were definitely revealed to them, and the full assurance that the sources presented correct material for their use could come only from God.

As far as the question of whether other spirits than God can establish this sort of contact with the minds of men is concerned, it should be noted that God sometimes employed angels in bringing these revelations to men. John, in the book of Revelation, speaks several times of such an angelic agent who brought God's revelation to him (Rev. 1:1; 17:1; 21:9; 22:8). The annunciation of the birth of John the Baptist to Zacharias and of the birth of Jesus to Mary by the angel Gabriel are well-known examples of angelic visitations and predictions (Luke 1:11-37). The appearance of the angel to the shepherds at Bethlehem after the birth of Jesus is an example of revelation of past events through the agency of angels. Many similar examples could be cited from both Old and New Testament time.

All of these biblical statements remind us that there is an unseen spiritual realm beyond the physical, material and visible world we see around us. It is also clear that God and the angels can in some mysterious way establish contact with human beings. God and angels can and did appear to men in visible form and were able to communicate with men.

While there are, therefore, in the Bible countless examples of supernatural knowledge, not only of religious truths but also of concrete historical events, yet a question which is not so clearly answered in Scripture concerns the ability of men to gain supernatural knowledge of secret things without the help of God. Can and do Satan and the evil angels make their presence known and felt? Are they able to communicate what they have come to know through their superior though limited intelligence? Are they able to help human beings predict the future? These are the questions that are involved when we deal with unlawful divination.

There can be no doubt in the mind of a Bible-believing Christian that the devil is able to communicate with men. He spoke through the serpent in the garden of Eden (Gen. 3:1-5). While we do not have a detailed description of the means employed by the devil in the temptation of Jesus, yet Jesus and the devil carried on a conversation with each other. Whether this was by way of mental communication or audible speech the Bible does not explain.

4

Whether the devil appeared in a visible form or not can also not be determined. But the text clearly speaks of it as an actual historical event. When we come to the subject of devil possession in a later chapter more evidence of some sort of communication between men and devils will be presented.

MENTAL TELEPATHY

Another question that cannot be left out of consideration is the possibility that there are powers within the human mind which are as yet not fully understood but which make it possible for certain persons to transcend the limits of space and time. Seemingly reliable witnesses who do not seek to deal with the unseen forces of the spirit world testify to occurrences that seem to indicate that it is sometimes possible to be aware of events that have happened in the past or that are happening far away without any empirical source of the awareness and even to have some remarkably exact premonitions of future events. Scientists who are confronted with evidence of such occurrences generally explain them as being evidence for the existence of such as yet little understood mental capacities, which are natural but paranormal, and found in a highly developed form only in a few exceptional people.

HOW SHALL WE JUDGE?

When we deal with occult divination phenomena it needs to be said that much fortune-telling is fraud, clever guesswork, or pure imagination. Most fortune-telling is so vague and general that it is very easy to find something that will seem to fit the prediction. The success of many fortune-tellers is based on the fact that they say things that people like to hear.

Nevertheless the Bible does indicate that not all divination is pure invention, but that it is possible for evil spirits to establish contact with and to inspire men. This is in some ways merely an extension and intensification of the devil's ability to influence our thinking, our will, our emotions and our actions. The witch of Endor, for example, correctly foretold the death of Saul. But even if the predictions spoken by false prophets do not come true, this, according to the Bible, does not mean that nothing more was involved than pure guesswork on the part of the prophet. The prophets of Ahab incorrectly foretold his victory at Ramoth-Gilead, but the Scriptural account indicates that they were inspired to make this prediction by a "lying spirit" (1 Kings 22:22). St. Paul also clearly teaches that many of the false doctrines taught in the church come from "seducing spirits" and that they are therefore "doctrines of devils" (1 Tim. 4:1). John implies the same thing when he says, "Dear friends, do not believe every spirit, but test the spirits to see whether they are from God, because many false prophets have gone out into the world" (1 John 4:1 NIV).

The Bible does not discuss in any detailed way the genuineness of such cases of occult divination. It does give us guidance on how to judge the truth or falsehood of the claim to revelation and how to evaluate the source from which the apparent revelation comes.

First of all, it should be borne in mind that exact and detailed knowledge of the future is possessed only by God. The prophet Isaiah challenges the prophets of false gods to foretell the future in order to demonstrate that the gods whom they serve are real. He writes,

Bring in your idols to tell us what is going to happen. Tell us what the former things were, so that we may consider them and know their final outcome. Or declare to us the things to come, tell us what the future holds, so that we may know that you are gods (Isa. 41:22,23 NIV).

God Himself through the prophet Isaiah makes the claim that He is the only God there is, because He is the only one who can correctly foretell what the future has in store (Isa. 44:6-8).

God does not say in any such passages that isolated predictions of false prophets may not come true. The claim He makes for Himself is that *all* of His prophecies are correct. Isaiah writes, "Seek ye out the book of the Lord and read. No one of these shall fail, none shall want her mate" (Isa. 34:16). That is why the New Testament so often says that the Scriptures *must* be fulfilled. No prophecy of Scripture can fail. If it seems to us that it has not come true, that can only mean that we have not understood it correctly. For example, modern theologians often say that Jesus was mistaken when He said that some of His disciples would not die before the kingdom of God would come in a powerful way. Modern theology, as well as some fundamentalistic theologians, teach that the kingdom of God is a perfect social order in which justice and mercy and peace will prevail all over the world. If that definition is correct, then, of course, the prediction is wrong. But the Bible clearly teaches that the kingdom of God comes when men in their hearts accept the message of the Gospel and become believers in Jesus Christ. When the Christian church was established over almost all of the known world before the apostles died, the kingdom of God had indeed come "with power" (Mark 9:1).

Since *all* of God's predictions come true, the failure of a prediction clearly demonstrates that it did not come from God. Moses told the children of Israel that they should not believe prophets who were not sent by God even if they claimed a divine mission for themselves. When the children of Israel then asked how they could know whether such a claim was false, Moses said, "When a prophet speaketh in the name of the Lord, if the thing follow not, nor come to pass, that is the thing which the Lord hath not spoken, but the prophet hath spoken it presumptuously; thou shalt not be afraid of him" (Deut. 18:22).

When diviners or seers therefore claim that their predictions are 75 per cent correct, this may seem impressive to some people, and it may at times be true that some predictions seem to find remarkable fulfillment. Yet a claim such as this is also an admission of error in 25 percent of the cases. Even one error would demonstrate that the fortune-teller does not speak for God and does not receive revelations from God.

Another test recommended in the Bible deals with the content of the pronouncements of fortune-tellers. In Deut. 13 Moses tells the children of Israel that if a prophet whose predictions come true tries to mislead them into a false religion, this is clear proof that he is a wicked man who deserves to die. When diviners, therefore, clearly teach things at variance with the Scriptures, this, too, is proof that they are servants of the devil.

More will be said about the sinfulness of divination later in this chapter.

ASTROLOGY

Probably the most popular form of divination in the world today is astrology, which is also often called the first step toward involvement in the occult. Of the 1700 or so daily newspapers in America over 1200 carry regular astrology columns, and the same practice is followed by many of the popular magazines. It is estimated that over $150,000,000 is spent per year on personal horoscopes,[4] that more than 10,000 men and women in America make their living by casting horoscopes and that 175,000 part-time practitioners of astrology are active in the United States.[5] Magazines devoted wholly to astrology, *Horoscope* and *American Astrology*, each have about a half million subscribers.[6]

Astrology is the art of predicting the future on the basis of the belief that the stars to a greater or lesser degree control or at least influence the character, the lives, and the destinies of men and nations.

The origin of astrology is hidden in the distant past. It is, however, generally agreed that its beginnings are found in Babylonia. When the New English Bible calls the wise men from the east "astrologers" it evidently does so on the premise that all the wise men from that area of the world were practitioners of astrology, and at least one German critic of the New Testament, Ethelbert Stauffer of Erlangen, has suggested that it was astrological doctrine that formed the basis of the conviction of the wise men that the king of the Jews had been born.[7] Stauffer says that in the summer of 7 B.C. Jupiter and Saturn were in conjunction in the sign of the Fishes and he writes,

> Jupiter was regarded as the star of the ruler of the universe, and the constellation of the Fishes was the sign of the last days. In the East Saturn was considered to be the planet of Palestine. If Jupiter encountered Saturn in the sign of the Fishes, it could only mean that the ruler of the last days would appear in Palestine. Such were the passages that prompted the Magi of Matthew 2, 2 to go to Jerusalem.[8]

Strangely enough, Stauffer believes that in this way he has demonstrated by the use of the historical-critical method that, as he says, "the star of Bethlehem too, is a historical fact."[9]

The basis of all astrological prediction is the zodiac, a word derived from the Greek word for "animal." The zodiac is an imaginary belt in the sky about fifteen degrees of arc wide with the ecliptic, or the apparent path of the sun, in the center of the belt.

The zodiac is divided into twelve sections, or "houses," each of which is named after a constellation which occupies or "governs" its house. These constellations are also called the "signs" of the zodiac. The whole belt of the zodiac moves around the earth once each year, so that each house occupies a position on the eastern horizon at sunrise for approximately one month, or, as it may be

8

SIGNS OF THE ZODIAC

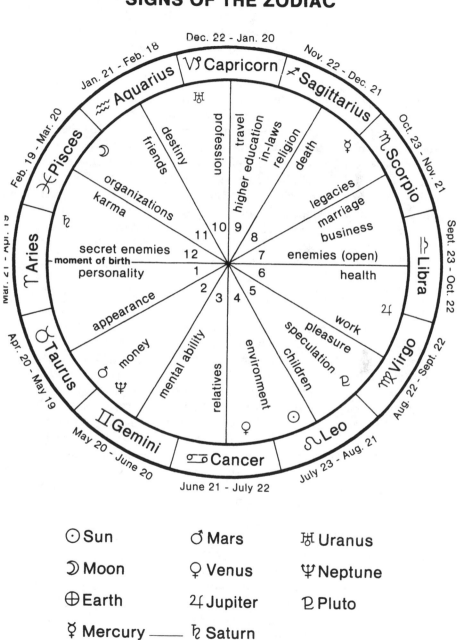

⊙ Sun   ♂ Mars   ♅ Uranus

☽ Moon   ♀ Venus   ♆ Neptune

⊕ Earth   ♃ Jupiter   ♇ Pluto

☿ Mercury —— ♄ Saturn

stated in another way, it takes the sun approximately one month to move from one house to another. The planets likewise move from one house to another at varying rates. Each planet is said to be "at home" in two houses and the sun and moon in one house each.

A horoscope is constructed on the basis of the position of the planets in the various houses at the moment of a person's birth. The most important astrological influence is that of the sun and one's astrological sign is determined by the position of the sun at the moment of birth. Lesser influences proceed from the moon and the planets. A horoscope is cast only after the exact position of the sun, moon, and the planets has been established (see the natal chart). Not only the position of the various planets in the houses is important but also their position in relation to each other. Planets are said to be in conjunction when they are situated in the same house within five degrees of each other. They are in opposition when they are six houses or 180 degrees apart, squared when they are three houses or 90 degrees apart; they form a sextile when they are two signs or 60 degrees apart and a trine when they are four signs or 120 degrees apart.

The rules for constructing a horoscope are very ancient, although astrologers have found it necessary to make some adjustments because since the rules were first laid down, three new planets have been discovered. The first point considered in all horoscopes is the position of the sun at the time of the candidate's birth. If the sun was in the house of the lion, for example, he will move with catlike grace and have as his most striking physical characteristic a heavy head of hair reminiscent of a lion's mane. One text on astrology says, "Leos love to be the center of attention and are driven by a desire to be in command."[10] For those who would like to test the accuracy of those statements it might be mentioned that Leos are people born between July 23 and August 21. If a bald-headed man is found among Leos, this can always be explained by saying that "the stars impel but do not compel." On the other hand, every Leo with a heavy head of hair will be tempted to believe that the system has some scientific basis.

The basic activity of the astrologer has remained unchanged since biblical times. The word "astrologer" is used eight times in the King James version, once in Isaiah and seven times in Daniel. The word translated "astrologer" in the Daniel passages really means "enchanter" or "magician." But the Isaiah passage (47:13) is most interesting. The KJ translation says, "Let now the astrologers, the stargazers, the monthly prognosticators, stand up, and save thee from these things that shall come upon thee." Literally the "astrologers" are "those who divide the heavens," which in this context clearly refers to the houses of the zodiac. The "stargazers" are those who observe the position of the stars in these divisions of the heavens. The "monthly prognosticators" are literally "those who give knowledge for the month," again an obvious reference to the fact that the sun spends approximately one month in each house of the zodiac every year.

The reading of the various rules for casting horoscopes will confirm the opinion that it is amazing what people are willing to believe just as long as it is not taught in the Bible. For example, although it is obvious that a connection is made between the zodiac sign of the Lion and the characteristics of those born when the sun is in the house of the Lion, it would certainly appear that the naming of the constellation is so arbitrary that the stars making up that constellation could just as readily have been named the "Lamb."

Moreover, the scientific fact is that people born between July 23 and August 21 are not born while the sun is in Leo. The sun arrives at the eastern horizon on March 21 a little earlier each year and therefore does not remain in the same house on the same date. This phenomenon is known as the precession of the equinoxes. In 25,800 years the sun will actually move through all the twelve houses on March 21,[11] which means that the sun will rise on March 21 in the same house for about 2,140 years and then will rise for the same length of time in the previous house of the zodiac. For people born in the last two thousand years the zodiacal signs have all been wrong. People classified as Aries, for example, who are born between March 21 and April 19, are not born while the sun is in the house of Aries but in the house of Pisces. This will no longer be true of those born on those dates in the future, for during the so-called Age of Aquarius the first day of spring will come while the sun is in the house of Aquarius. Thus those who are classified by astrologers as Aries will actually be Aquarians.

Moreover, the boundaries of the houses are so ill-defined that astrologers are not really sure in what year the sun will begin to rise in Aquarius on the first day of spring. Some say it began in

1904, others date its beginning 1936 or 1962, while still others insist that it has not yet begun.[12]

While astrologers are not sure just when the new age of Aquarius will be ushered in, if it has not already begun, they all seem to agree that a new star age means a new beginning for the earth. They often point to the fact that Jesus was born near the beginning of the Piscean age, or age of fishes.[13] When the new age of Aquarius begins new types of government, new forms of worship and new philosophies will come into existence. Sybil Leek, for example, says that in the age of Aquarius, "There will be a completely new set of values — moral, religious, personal, and national."[14] Some astrologers evidently believe that Christianity will go out of existence and that humanism will be the religion of the future. When we compare this pronouncement made by numerous promoters of astrology with the teaching of the Bible that the Word of God will endure forever, the spirit that inspires such doctrine is easily identified.

There are other difficulties involved in this whole theory that the stars influence life on earth. Why should only the constellations in the narrow band of the zodiac exercise such influence? Moreover, in eastern countries where astrology is even more widely practiced than in the west, other symbols are used which have different meanings from those given to the various signs of the zodiac by those who follow the Ptolemaic system.

It is also strange that the moment of birth should be chosen as a determining factor in constructing a personal horoscope. It would surely seem that the moment of conception would be more reasonable if there were any truth in the system.

In spite of all these difficulties astrologers insist that their art is a science. They point to the fulfillment of their prophecies as proof for their claims. When these claims are examined, however, they often demonstrate rather the folly of the art. As an impressive instance of the fulfillment of an astrological prediction, one astrologer cited the magazine *Astrology Today* which prior to the assassination of Pres. Kennedy printed a horoscope for that November in which it was said, "The powerful Mars influence incites much social unrest of the sort that erupts blindly into retaliative violence."[15] As a specific prediction of the Kennedy assassination those words clearly leave much to be desired. Moreover, they are so general that dozens of events that happened during that November, or for that matter, during any month of any year, could be cited as a fulfillment.

At the beginning of 1976 I noticed that the copy of the *National Enquirer* of January 6, 1976, displayed in the supermarket, contained astrological predictions for that year. Because I knew that I would be writing on this subject in September of 1976, I bought a copy and placed the astrology page into my files. By September it was already clear that many predictions were inaccurate. When the predictions were again examined at the end of 1976, it was even clearer that the astrology page published twelve months before could only be described as a disaster. The article contained about sixty predictions. Of the sixty, thirty-nine or almost 66 per cent were completely and definitely false. Twenty I was unable to check because I did not have adequate information, or because they are so vague that it was difficult to decide what would be considered a fulfillment of the prophecy. For example, one psychic predicted that Caroline Kennedy would become "involved in politics" and "in a bitter fight with her family." Another predicted that Mary Tyler Moore's career would "take a skid." In the sixty predictions there was only one of which I know that it had an element of truth in it. That was the prediction that Henry Kissinger would lose both his job and his wife. The wording of the first half of the statement seems to imply that he would be removed from office by the president and that this would take place in 1976. Strictly interpreted the first part of the prediction could be classified as false, but it is not counted among the thirty-nine mentioned above, because it is possible to argue that for all practical purposes Kissinger lost his job with the election of a Democratic president in November of 1976. The second half of the statement was, of course, also false.

It might be of some interest to note some of the more easily checked predictions. Various seers foretold that in 1976
   1) President Ford would not run because of serious family problems;
   2) A new war would break out in the Mid-East;
   3) Nelson Rockefeller would become president;
   4) Huge gold deposits would be discovered in Colorado with a "Klondike like" gold rush;
   5) Pope Paul would resign;

6) Several attempts would be made on Ronald Reagan's life;
7) President Ford would be shot in the left shoulder or arm while attending a convention in a western state;
8) Queen Elizabeth would abdicate;
9) Richard Nixon would begin a slow climb back to political power, beginning with a behind-the-scenes bid for the governorship of California; and that
10) Susan Ford would be married in the spring.

Other studies of astrological predictions have shown the same disappointing results. William Petersen cites a research project in which the predictions of leading astrologers for one day were compared, and his conclusion was "that if you want to keep your faith in astrology, you better not compare one against the other."[16] Walker Knight says that "when astrologers are followed up, almost complete disappointment results."[17]

Isolated instances of fulfilled astrological predictions can truthfully be cited. But if dozens of horoscopes are cast dealing with the same person, some of them are bound to be correct. Many astrologers claim that they predicted President Kennedy's death. Kurt Koch says that prior to November of 1963 one horoscope predicted the president's impending death, another predicted his reelection in the following year, and still another that he would be forced to resign in 1964 for reasons of health.[18] Under such conditions, fulfilled predictions ought to occasion no surprise.

On the other hand, scientific studies have clearly demonstrated the folly of astrology. Paul Couderc, of the Paris Observatory, investigated the birth dates of 2,817 musicians to see whether any pattern could be discovered that would show a correlation between the signs of the zodiac and musical ability. According to astrological theory there ought to be such a correlation, but Couderc concluded that the position of the sun has no influence whatever. He found that musicians are born throughout the year on a chance basis. Couderc's conclusion was that the value of astrology is "zero."[19] A similar study of the birth dates of scientists listed in *Who's Who* produced the same results, and the conclusion arrived at was that the birth dates of scientists are just as random as those of the rest of the population.[20]

Yet, in spite of everything, millions of people believe in the system. On May 24, 1976, *U.S. News and World Report* published an article on the subject which alluded to a Gallup Poll that showed that about 32,000,000 people in America took astrology seriously. Sad to say, the pollsters discovered that as many churchgoers as others said that they believed in astrology.[21]

Even many leading theologians, including also Lutheran theologians, have seen no harm in the casting of horoscopes. Some have even advocated and practiced the art themselves. Philip Melanchthon and Martin Chemnitz, for example, believed that astrology was a scientific discipline. Martin Luther, however, ridiculed the practice. Although he is quoted in the *Tischreden* as saying that it was invented by the devil, yet in his commentary on Genesis he says that he has no great objection to astrological prediction because "geniuses must be allowed their pastime."

Nevertheless, having said that, he goes on to say,

> So far as this matter is concerned, however, I shall never be convinced that astrology should be numbered among the sciences. And I shall adhere to this opinion because astrology is completely without proof. The appeal to experience has no effect on me. All the astrological experiences are purely individual cases. The experts have taken note of and recorded only those instances which did not fail, but they took no note of the rest of the attempts, where they were wrong and the results which they predicted as certain did not follow. Aristotle says that one swallow does not make a spring, and so I do not believe that from such partial observations a science can be established. Hunters have a similar saying: A hunt may be carried on every day, but the hunt is not successful every day. The very same thing may be said of the astrologers and their predictions, because very often what they predict *fails* to come true.
>
> Even if there were something sure about these predictions, what stupidity it is to be much concerned about the future! For granted that the future can be known through astrological predictions — if they are bad, ignorance of them is certainly better in many respects than knowledge of them, as Cicero also declares. An abiding fear of God and prayer are preferable to the fear of future events (LW, I, 45).

Luther also rejected the common interpretation that tried to justify the practice of astrology on the basis of the statement in the first chapter of Genesis which says that the sun and moon and stars were to serve as "signs." Luther says that these words must not be understood to mean that the sun and moon and stars exercise an influence over our destiny (St.L. III, 1147f).

We cannot defend men like Melanchthon and Chemnitz, who ought to have known better. Their acceptance of astrology is a weakness which can, at least in part, be traced to the culture in which they lived. In that culture astrology was not commonly recognized for what it really is, ignorant superstition at best, and a tool of the devil to undermine confidence in the government of God at worst.

Dr. Joyce Brothers explains the popularity of astrology by saying that "astrologers know what their clients want and they dish it out. This feeling is further reinforced by what psychologists call 'the self-fulfilling prophecy' — the likelihood that saying a thing is going to happen will actually bring it about."[22] It might be said also that much of what is written in the daily astrology columns is good advice. If a man is told that on a certain day it is especially important for him to be careful not to let his temper get out of hand he can hardly go wrong in following that counsel. *Time* magazine some years ago pointed out how difficult it is to demonstrate the incorrectness of many astrological assertions by saying, "Break a leg when your astrologer told you the signs were good, and he can congratulate you on escaping what might have happened had the signs been bad."[23] It has been said that successful astrologers are good psychologists.

When this whole business is examined just on the basis of human reason alone, we find that, even if we can not fully agree with the judgment on astrology pronounced by the Astronomical Society, yet it is basically true, as the Society said in 1949, that "Whatever lies behind the title of astrology . . . is nothing more than a mixture of superstition, duplicity, and business."[24] The Roman poet Ennius was right when he said that horoscopes cost one drachma each and are one drachma too expensive.

Some astrologers admit this openly or indicate unconsciously that they are aware of it. Johann Kepler, the famed astronomer, practiced astrology because his livelihood depended on it; but he said,

Astronomy is the wise mother and astrology is her

whoring little daughter, selling herself to any and every client willing and able to pay so as to maintain her wise mother alive.[25]

And in the *Milwaukee Journal* an astrologer who claims that he is consulted by many important leaders in business and politics said that many people would be shocked if they knew how many decisions are guided by the stars. He confessed that he himself was frightened at the thought. If he truly had the confidence in his craft that he professes to have, he would not need to fear the consequences.[26]

ANCIENT DIVINATION

While astrology is the most popular form of divination practiced today, there are countless other ways in which men seek hidden knowledge in ways that are unlawful. Many of these methods, like astrology, are thousands of years old and are referred to already in the Bible. Ezekiel, for example, refers to one of the most common types of Mesopotamian divination when he says that the king of Babylon "looked in the liver" (Ezek. 21:21). Close examination of the liver of a sacrificed animal was made the basis of predictions concerning the king, and clay livers have been found in Mesopotamia that were used to teach the art. The Greeks called this practice hepatoscopy and they also practiced it. The same passage in Ezekiel says that the king shook the arrows, a reference to another mode of divination among both Babylonians and Greeks. The Roman custom of consulting augurs and *haruspices,* who divined by examining the entrails of animals as well as the flight and feeding of birds, is a similar practice. It is very likely that Moses was referring to activities similar to these when he spoke of observers of times, enchanters, and charmers in Deuteronomy 18: 10,11. Keil-Delitzsch says that in these verses Moses groups together all the words used in Hebrew for the different ways of discovering what the future had in store.

ROD AND PENDULUM

Similar practices are still prevalent today. One ancient mode of divination still very common in Germany today, according to Kurt Koch, is the use of a rod or a pendulum. They are used in various ways to point out the answer to the question being asked. In using the rod or pendulum to discover information useful to sick people, for example, the rod is passed over the body until it responds and points to the area that is supposedly affected. The pendulum is used in the same way until it begins to circle over the affected organ. Sometimes instead of passing the rod or pendulum over the body itself the diviner uses a chart of the body instead. Others use the rod or the pendulum in a similar way to select the proper medicine from a group of remedies or drugs. In some respects this method is similar to dowsing for water, of which a little more will be said later.

CARD LAYING

Cartomancy or card laying is more common in America. While some fortune-tellers who employ this method of divination use a regular card deck, it is more common for those who take this business seriously to use the Tarot.

The Tarot is a deck of cards that was invented in Italy early in the fourteenth century. A full deck consists of 78 cards, which are divided into the Lesser Arcana (or Trumps Minor) and the Greater Arcana (or Trumps Major). The Lesser Arcana is very similar to a bridge deck except that it has a fourth face card called the page. The Greater Arcana consists of 21 numbered face cards, many of which depict religious symbolism, and one "fool" or joker.

The cards are shuffled until the practitioner "feels" intuitively that they have been shuffled enough, after which a number of cards are laid out in one of several standard patterns. Each card has its own significance and, as in astrology, the position and combination of the cards has special meaning.

Advocates of fortune-telling by means of cards say that significant readings are given only if the reader enters into a trance state and it appears at times that we are dealing here with something that comes very close to possession by the devil,[27] and one writer with a favorable attitude toward card laying says that the Tarot cards "have a special magic of their own as any sensitive person who has handled a pack can perceive."[28] Kurt Koch says that some forms of card laying are based on genuine mediumistic abilities. He tells of one fortune-teller who under questioning admitted that when she was actively in the process of telling fortunes she found herself controlled by a strange power that actually forced her to sav things of which she had no previous knowledge.[29] Merrill Unger also says that "mediumistic abilities are often present in card-laying,"[30] and we shall have more to say of this when we discuss the subject of spiritism.

I CHING

Another type of fortune-telling becoming more popular in America is I Ching, or the *Book of Changes,* translated from the Chinese. In using the I Ching, Chinese people work with fifty yarrow stalks, but in America usually three coins are used. The coins are tossed six times and according to the way the coins fall either a broken or solid line is drawn until you have six lines one above another (e.g. ☰☰☰). This same pattern will also be found at the beginning of one of the chapters of the book. The chapters are very short and very obscure, but those who use it find the answers to their questions in them. In some ways it is similar to the sinful practice of pointing blindfolded to passages in the Bible to find guidance.

PALMISTRY or CHIROMANCY

A far more common and well-known type of divination is palmistry or chiromancy, telling fortunes by examining the hands. This is also a very ancient practice.

It would seem that palmistry operates with principles and rules similar to those used by astrologers but its connection with paganism is even clearer. The user of astrology may speak of Jupiter, Mars, and Venus exclusively in terms of the planets which bear those names, but palmistry still uses the name of Apollo as the name of the sun. Just as astrology depends on the position of the sun, moon and the five planets which bear the name of old Roman gods, so various areas of the hand are named after the gods Mercury, Apollo, Saturn and Venus. The patterns of interpretation are very similar to those followed in astrology. For example, the little finger is assigned to Mercury, the god of travel. If the fleshy area in the palm just below the little finger, called the mount of Mercury, is pronounced, this indicates a love of travel. The shape and length of the fingers, the conformation of various areas of the palms, and the various lines of the hand are examined as a basis for the reading. But again it might be said that the more successful chiromantists are those who exhibit mediumistic gifts, that is, fortune-tellers who seem to have established some kind of contact with evil spirits.

PSYCHOMETRY

A few words might also be said about psychometry. Those who practice this type of divination operate with some object worn or used by the person concerning whom information is desired. Occasionally we come across newspaper articles concerning psychics who have found missing persons or identified murderers in this way. Kurt Koch tells of a diviner who was able by the use of the man's socks to point to the exact spot where the body of a suicide could be found.[31] But the device is also used to describe the characteristics of the person involved or to see something in his or her past, present, or future. For what it is worth, it might be mentioned in this connection that Kurt Koch testifies that he met a clairvoyant in Switzerland who used psychometric powers and whose statements were 100 per cent accurate. For example, he could diagnose illnesses correctly if an object belonging to the sick person was placed before him. The Dutch psychic, Peter Hurkos, makes extensive use of this device in his work with police departments.

ONEIROMANCY

Oneiromancy, or the interpretation of dreams, is another type of divination that is very popular.

God sometimes used dreams to reveal the future to men. The dreams of Joseph (Gen. 37:5-11), of Pharaoh's butler and baker (Gen. 40:5-23), of Pharaoh himself (Gen. 41:1-36), and of Nebuchadnezzar (Dan. 2:1-45) are well-known to all Bible readers. Even in New Testament times God employed this means of revealing His will. Joseph was warned by God in a dream to flee to Egypt (Matt. 2:13) and the wise men were told in this same way not to return to Herod (Matt. 2:12). There are in addition to these many other examples of the same thing (cp., e.g. Gen. 20:3, 31:11; 31:24; 1 Kings 3:5; Dan. 7:1).

While God said that He would speak through dreams (Num. 12:6), yet it is also stated clearly in the Bible that dreams, in general, are not reliable guides to life or for the future. They are easily employed by false prophets to deceive men. Jeremiah speaks of the prophets who cause God's people to forget God's name "by their dreams which they tell" (Jer. 23:27). God Himself, in that connection, says, "The prophet that hath a dream, let him tell a dream; and he that hath my word, let him speak my word faithfully. What is the chaff to the wheat?"

There is no doubt that there have been remarkable fulfillments of dreams also in our day. Whether, however, those dreams came from God or from the devil, or whether they were accidental agreements between dreams and reality is not so easy to determine, nor is it necessary to do so.

We must admit that God can give revelations through dreams. It is, moreover, not easily denied that the devil can also mimic God here. Because it is so easy for the devil or his servants to mislead men by this means and because God has forbidden it, Christians will not seek out fortune-tellers who specialize in oneiromancy. Moreover, in evaluating their own dreams they can follow no better advice than that given by God through Jeremiah, "He that hath a dream, let him tell a dream; and he that hath my word, let him speak my word faithfully." Any dream that contradicts the Word of God or that has a tendency to lead men away from trust in God must be characterized as being from the devil.

There are also many other types of divination which we can not discuss. Crystal gazing, numerology, and the reading of tea leaves or coffee grounds are some of the more familiar. All of these methods may at times seem to work, especially when they are employed by people with psychic gifts, or mediumistic abilities.

CLAIRVOYANCE

A word should, however, be said about clairvoyance or what is commonly called "second sight," the ability to see more or less vividly things or events that are far away in space or time. In many cases this would appear to be very closely related to mental telepathy. It often occurs spontaneously in people who have no desire to traffic with the occult.

"Clairvoyance" seems to be related to valid prophetic gifts. The prophets often "saw" the events of the future which they described. They were, therefore, often called "seers," or "men who see," and their prophecies are described as "visions" (e.g. Isa. 1:1).

However, it is a gift which is easily abused in the interest of divination. Jeane Dixon is a case in point. She uses some of the methods described above, astrology, dreams, a crystal ball or a deck of cards, but often does not look at the cards and only holds them in her hand for the "vibrations."She claims to have had a number of "visions." She says, however, that while the visions are never wrong, she is sometimes mistaken in her interpretation of what the visions mean. It should be obvious that obscure visions without divinely guided interpretation are useless as a guide for the future. This is also demonstrated by the dreams of Pharaoh, which were useless until interpreted by Joseph, who said that the interpretation could only come from God.

I suppose, however, that a number of us could cite cases in which such clairvoyant experience came to people who could hardly be accused of being involved with the occult world of evil spirits. A very close friend of mine, while waiting for a plane in the O'Hare terminal near Chicago, saw his dog jump up at him and heard him barking at the same moment that the dog died at his home.

Such experiences make it very difficult to draw the line between psychological mysteries and occult practices. But the ease with which some people pass from such passive experiences to involvement with the occult ought to teach us to exercise great caution in this area.

WATER DOWSING

A related practice is that of dowsing, or divining for water. This, too, is a very old practice. In ancient Rome dowsers or "water witches" were called *aquileges*. It seems rather well established that there are people who have the ability to walk over an area with a forked stick in their hands and locate water under the ground. Some of them can even tell exactly how deep the water is below the surface. I have been told on rather good authority that at one of our Lutheran high schools several attempts were made to drill a well without success. Finally one of the board members took his niece, who was a dowser, to the high school grounds one evening, and today the school has a good supply of water from a well drilled at the spot marked by the girl.

In my younger years I used to ridicule all such stories as nonsense, but the evidence pointing to the success of this method of finding water seems to be overwhelming. Up to 1975, for example, the town of New Sharon in Maine suffered from a chronic shortage of water. The town spent $180,000 for geologic studies and drilled several wells that produced nothing. Finally, in desperation the city fathers hired a dowser for $500. Today, as a result of his efforts, the town has all the water it can use.[32]

I would find it very difficult to condemn the practice. Certainly God's name is not being taken in vain and no evil spirit powers are being summoned to give their aid. And yet when I read that there are dowsers who can hold the divining rod over a map and locate water in this way hundreds of miles away, I am not so sure that in at least some cases there are occult powers involved. Kurt Koch finds a very close connection between dowsing and the use of the divining rod for fortune-telling. Yet he says that in his pastoral counseling he has not found any evidence of any psychological disturbance that has resulted from dowsing on a purely physical level.[33] Since Koch holds that involvement with the occult always has a tendency to bring psychological disturbance with it, it would seem that there may be some natural forces involved. This can hardly be said, however, if the dowsing is done over a map or chart.

THE DANGERS INVOLVED

Nor can it be said of truly occult practices. Kurt Koch, who seems to be well aware of the need to avoid credulity in the area of the occult, has cited literally hundreds of cases in which tragedy, psychological disturbances, and even insanity have resulted from occult practices. He tells, for example, of a young German mother with two children who was told by two card layers that her husband who was missing in action was dead. After the second visit she killed herself and her children with gas. The next day her husband came home from a Russian prison camp.[34]

One story like that, of course, does not make a case. However, even those who are heartily in favor of divination recognize that such events are not at all unexpected results of fortune-telling. In doing research on this subject I read two books of instruction in the art of divination, and both of them warn against revealing what is learned from card laying or other methods of divination if it will have a tendency to upset the person having his fortune told. One of the authors writes, "To predict death, illness, accidents, and catastrophe can cause many to worry unnecessarily."[36] He advises, therefore, that in such cases the diviner should not tell the "truth" learned by divination.

The same author speaks of the danger that threatens the fortune-teller. He writes, "Because of the dangers that can attend trance meditation, it is well, to begin with, to submit to direction from a virtuous and well-instructed adept."

A Christian student of the occult quotes a German psychologist who said, "We can see how dangerous it (dabbling in the occult) is by the way in which serious psychic disturbances, a fear of life, despair and dérangement are produced by it in sensitive people. Astrology paralyzes initiative and powers of judgment. It stupefies and encourages shallowness. It molds the personality into receiving an underground movement that thrives on platitudes."[37]

THE SINFULNESS OF DIVINATION

Christians, however, really do not need to prove the dangerous nature of divination. Nor is it necessary for them to answer the question of whether it is fraudulent or real. Even those who advocate the practice admit that there are many charlatans who have given divination a bad name. And those who seem to have truly "miraculous" powers of prediction do not claim inerrancy for themselves. The many mistakes made by even the most successful psychics demonstrate beyond question that this type of prophecy is not from God. As we have already seen, when the children of Israel asked how they could distinguish a false prophet from a spokesman of the Lord, Moses told them that the prophet whose predictions do not come true is not from God (Deut. 18:22).

On the other hand, if the prophecies do not come true, this does not prove that the fortune-teller is a complete fraud and dissembler. The devil is the father of lies and he tells the truth or lies as it suits his purposes to do so. The lying spirits in the mouth of the prophets of Ahab led him to his death (1 Kings 22:1-38).

What children of God need to remember is that all divination is directly forbidden by God (Deut. 18:10,11; Isa. 44:25; Lev. 19:26). It is a violation of the first commandment. If the name of God is employed for such divination, it is also an offense against the second commandment. The Christian believer who knows that God has loved him with an everlasting love in Christ and who says, "My times are in Thy hand," does not need the assurance offered by those who are charlatans at best and direct agents of the old evil foe at worst. Astrology at least made sense when heathen men believed that the planets were intelligent gods who could influence the lives of men. Today it is only another example of the irrationality of unbelief, and at yet the same time a form of idolatry that is every bit as evil as open paganism. Merrill Unger is right when he says, "The upsurge in astrological interest is unmistakable evidence of moral and social decay."[38]

The kind of interest in the future displayed by those who use divination to discover what lies before them manifests a lack of trust in the wisdom of God who has revealed to us what we need to know and who promises that all things will work together for our good. Divination, however, is not only destructive of faith. The attitude toward morality that is inculcated by it is destructive of Christian living. When one reads the advice of the astrological columns it becomes clear very quickly that the morality of astrologers is pure pragmatism. The fundamental questions that are always involved are, "Will it benefit me?" The Christian, however, ought to ask, "Is it right?" The astrologers often excuse their mistakes by saying that "the stars impel, but do not compel," and that astrology is only an aid to guiding us in making our decisions. God has given us the only guide we need. In questions of morals, He has given us the Law. In questions that deal purely with decisions concerning this present life he has given us human reason. Astrology subverts both.

Divination in all its forms is therefore to be avoided by all Christians. We do not drink poison to see what it tastes like. In the same way we ought to be on our guard against any kind of involvement in these practices, even if it is done only for entertainment. To the argument that it is just in fun or for curiosity's sake Kurt Koch answers, "Whether it is out of ignorance or curiosity, whether as a joke or in all seriousness, when I release the catch on a hand grenade, the result is always the same."[39] In the Lord's commands against all manner of fortune-telling we have only another evidence of His love which desires that we avoid all those things that can in the end only bring grief and suffering with them.

SOURCES
Chapter I

1. Rudolf Bultmann and others, *Kerygma and Myth,* edited by Hans Werner Bartsch, translated by Reginald H. Fuller, New York, Harper Torchbooks, 1961 (German edition, 1948), p. 4.

2. Jules Michelet, *Satanism and Witchcraft, a Study in Medieval Superstition,* tr. by A. R. Allinson, New York, The Citadel Press, 1939. (note on back cover).

3. Julio Caro Baroja, *The World of the Witches,* tr. by O. N. V. Glendenning, Chicago, University of Chicago Press, 1965, p. 131 (published in Spanish in 1961).

4. Edmond C. Gruss, *Cults and the Occult in the Age of Aquarius,* Grand Rapids, Baker, 1974, p. 76.

5. Merrill Unger, *Demons in the World Today,* Wheaton, Ill., Tyndale Publishers, 1971, p. 60. See also Wm. J. Petersen *Those Curious New Cults,* New Canaan, Conn., Keats Publishing Inc., 1975, p. 22.

6. Wm J. Petersen, op. cit., p. 22.

7. Ethelbert Stauffer, *Jesus and His Story,* tr. by Richard and Clara Winston, New York, Alfred Knopf, 1960, pp. 32ff.

8. Ibid., p. 33.

9. Ibid., p. 34.

10. Rod Davies, *How To Tell Fortunes,* New York, Pinnacle Books, 1976, p. 145f.

11. *Life Nature Library, The Earth,* by Arthur Beiser and the Edition of Life, New York, Time Incorporated, 1962, p. 13.

12. Wm. J. Petersen, op. cit., p. 28.

13. Sybil Leek, *My Life in Astrology,* Englewood Cliffs, N. J., Prentice-Hall, 1972, p. 202.

    (I am surprised that in the extensive reading which I did on the subject I did not find one astrologer who pointed out the fact that the fish is a symbol of Christianity.)

14. Op. cit., p. 202.

15. Wm. J. Petersen, op. cit., p. 32.

16. Ibid., p. 28.

17. Walker L. Knight, *The Weird World of the Occult,* Wheaton, Ill., Tyndale House, 1972, p. 18.

18. Kurt E. Koch, *Christian Counselling and Occultism,* Grand Rapids, Kregel, 1972, pp. 97f.

19. John Warwick Montgomery, *Principalities and Powers,* Minneapolis, Bethany Fellowship, 1973, pp. 113f.

20. Petersen, op. cit., p. 30.

21. Op. cit., p. 74.

22. Quoted in Knight, op. cit., p. 17.

23. *Time,* March 21, 1969, p. 56.

24. Quoted in Petersen, op. cit., pp. 30f.

25. Kurt Koch, *Between Christ and Satan,* Grand Rapids, Kregel, 1962, p. 13.

26. *Milwaukee Journal,* July 25, 1976, *Insight Magazine,* p. 14.

27. Basil Ivan Rakoczi, *Foreseeing the Future,* New York, Harper and Row, 1973, p. 53.
28. Ibid., p. 36.
29. Kurt Koch, *Between Christ and Satan,* p. 21.
30. Op. cit., p. 63.
31. *Between Christ and Satan,* p. 32.
32. Emily and Per Ola D'Aulaire, "The Forked Stick Phenomenon," *Reader's Digest, May, 1976, p. 136.*
33. Kurt Koch, *Christian Counseling and Occultism,* Grand Rapids, Kregel, 1972, p. 104.
34. Ibid., p. 82f.
35. Rod Davies, op. cit., p. 11.
36. Rakoczi, op. cit., p. 53.
37. Petersen, op. cit. p. 30
38. Op. cit., p. 60.
39. *Christian Counselling and Occultism,* p. 83.

2

Magic and Witchcraft

"There shall not be found among you . . . an enchanter, or a witch, or a charmer . . . or a wizard . . . For all that do these things are an abomination unto the LORD."   Deut. 18:10-12.

Parapsychologists distinguish between two kinds of psychic phenomena and speak of them as being either of the Psi-Gamma or Psi-Kappa type. Psi-Gamma phenomena are those that involve paranormal knowledge, the name being derived from the Greek word "gignoskein" (to know). The various forms of divination, since they involve the acquisition of supposedly supernatural knowledge, belong under this classification. Psi-Kappa phenomena are those that involve some paranormal physical or psychical effect on people or things. The name of this second type is derived from the Greek word for "move" (kinein). The various forms of magic and witchcraft for the most part belong to this category, although many witches also practice divination.

In a general way it may be said that in the practice of genuine divination, as well as in true prophecy, some sort of contact is established between the spiritual forces in the universe and the mind of man. In the practice of witchcraft and magic an effort is made to bring some sort of spirit influence to bear on the world of matter.

The materialistic philosophy so prevalent in our time not only denies the existence of spirit beings but it assumes that even if such beings existed it would be impossible for them to exercise any influence on material things. According to this philosophy we live in a closed universe where everything that happens must have an adequate cause within the system, and all events result from the operation of the laws of nature. In such a view magic and witch-craft are excluded from the realm of possibility.

MAGIC AND MIRACLE

That we do not live in a closed universe where no spirit influence can be brought to bear on the material world is clearly demonstrated for a Christian believer by the miracles recorded in the Bible. Materialistic philosophy of course also denies the possibility of miracles. But no Bible-believing Christian can deny that miracles are possible.

In Old Testament times, according to the witness of Scripture, men who were especially appointed by God performed miracles as evidences of their divine mission, of the truthfulness of their claims, and of the authenticity of their message.

The number of miracles recorded in the Old Testament is rather limited and, according to the biblical record, there are only two short periods in Old Testament history when especially many miracles were performed. The first of these periods is the time of Moses and Joshua, when the first books of the Bible were produced. The second is the period of Elijah and Elisha, the first of a long and almost unbroken line of prophets. During the centuries from Moses to Elijah, it would seem that God revealed His will especially through the priests. But from the time of Elijah until the end of the Old Testament most revelations from God came through the prophets. It would seem therefore that miracles became especially numerous when God wished to indicate that He was about to employ a new method of dealing with men in His revelatory activity.

This conclusion seems to be substantiated when we come to the New Testament. The third great miracle period described in the Bible is the time of Jesus and the apostles. Jesus is the greatest of all the messengers of God to this world and the apostles were His specially ordained spokesmen. In Jesus God, who had in earlier times spoken through the prophets, spoke to men through His own Son (Heb. 1:1-3). He made the claim that He had come directly from God and He pointed to His miracles as proof for the validity of this claim (cp. e.g. John 10:22-38; 3:2). According to John's Gospel the miracles of the Savior were done to convince men that He was the Christ, the Son of God (John 20:30,31).

New Testament with the miracle of Jesus' birth. Both of these accounts testify to the reality of the contact between God, who is spirit, and the world of matter.

Jesus Himself is the greatest miracle of all. In the beginning God created man out of the dust of the ground. In Jesus God has become man. The miraculous character of Jesus Himself becomes especially clear in the so-called *personal miracles,* such as the virgin birth, the transfiguration, the resurrection, and the ascension into heaven.

Aside from the personal miracles, the "wondrous works" of Jesus may be described as belonging to one of four types of miracles.

1) The most common are the *healing miracles.* Of the thirty-six miracles described in some detail in the four Gospels, eighteen deal with the cure of illnesses or physical disabilities. The illnesses cured range from leprosy and paralysis to blindness and deafness. At least one of the men cured by Jesus was a man who had been born blind (John 9:1-7). In one case an ear that had been cut off was restored to its place (Luke 22:50).

2) There are three recorded cases of *resurrection* miracles, the young man of Nain (Luke 7:11), the daughter of Jairus (Matt. 9:23; Mark 5:38; Luke 8:49), and Lazarus of Bethany (John 11:43).

3) The *curing of demoniacs* must be viewed as distinct from the healing miracles. In the light of the common statement that in Jesus' time diseases generally were viewed as being due to the direct influence of demons it is significant to note that there are only six cases described in any detail that involve devil possession. Moreover, the New Testament itself distinguishes between devil possession and other illnesses or physical disabilities (Matt. 8:16).

4) From the point of view of modern science the so-called *nature miracles* are especially significant. These are miracles in which Jesus produces a supernatural effect on the course of the natural, material world. The changing of water into wine, the multiplication of the loaves and fishes at the feeding of the five thousand and the four thousand, the stilling of the tempest, Jesus' walking on the water, the coin in the fish's mouth, and the cursing of the fig tree are examples of this type of miracle.

Many modern theologians accept only the healing miracles as having some historical basis. The nature miracles are for the most part usually viewed as being completely impossible since they would involve a violation of the laws of nature. The resurrection miracles are spoken of as "exaggerated" accounts of healing miracles or pure invention, and devil possession is viewed as an impossibility. Many of the healing miracles, including the cure of demoniacs, are accepted as having some historical basis, but they are explained as psychological cures. Such an explanation of course implies that nothing supernatural really happened, but that all the supposed miracles, if they have any historical basis at all, can be explained as natural events for which there is a sufficient, even if unknown, cause in the material world.

What is really at issue here is the question of whether it is possible for supernatural events, contrary to the laws of nature, to happen. The denial of even the possibility of real supernatural occurrences lies at the root of much of the incredulity displayed by many modern theologians in regard to the nature miracles. However, anyone who accepts the Gospels as a truthful historical account of the life and work of Jesus and who takes this account at face value must admit that the occurrence of events for which there is no adequate cause in the natural world is possible.

In itself this does not necessarily imply that magic and witchcraft are ever genuinely supernatural. We do not know and perhaps can never know with absolute certainty whether it is possible for the devil and his angels to have a similar influence on the material world. We can not say *a priori* that the nature of the world makes such a thing unthinkable. But we may still ask whether, for example, the magicians of Pharaoh were actually able to duplicate the miracle of turning sticks into serpents or whether they were clever tricksters who could create the illusion that they had done so.

The Bible does not answer that question for us. The biblical statement "The magicians of Egypt did in like manner by their enchantments" (Exod. 7:11), does not necessarily imply that their productions were supernatural. The complete significance of the Hebrew word translated "magicians" is not known. It seems to denote a class of heathen Egyptian priests. The word translated "enchantments" is translated "secret arts" in the RSV, a translation which is possible. Modern commentators generally assume that the magicians were tricksters, but the simple words of the Bible do not make this self-evident. If they were nothing more than clever deceivers, why is it that they were not able to reproduce the turn-

ing of dust into lice? Why did they say, "This is the finger of God"
(Exod. 8:18,19)? It would certainly seem that the production of lice
from dust would be no more difficult and perhaps even easier than
the production of snakes and frogs. A much more logical place for
the magicians to fail, if they were nothing more than sleight of
hand artists, would be during the fifth plague in which the cattle
of Egypt became ill and died. It would seem also that if the account
is read without modern prejudices against the supernatural, the
words would be understood to mean that the magicians of Pharaoh were able to produce effects that could not be called forth by
natural means. But to make dogmatic assertions in either direction is not justified.

And even if we admit that the magicians possessed supernatural powers, we would still need to ask whether it is still possible for
men today to enlist the help of evil spirits to obtain results that
could not be obtained through the use of natural means? And
even if we grant that it is possible, as we surely must, this would
still not settle the question of whether it actually does happen.
This question also the Bible does not answer.

THE PURPOSE OF MIRACLES

Miracles serve a very real purpose in God's revelation to men.
When God came to Moses at the burning bush (Exod. 3 and 4) to
tell him to announce to Israel their impending deliverance from
the power of Pharaoh and their return to the promised land,
Moses was sure that the children of Israel would not believe what
he had to tell them. God then gave Moses the power to perform
three miracles and gave him the promise that these miracles, or
"signs," would cause the people to accept his message (Exod.
4:8,9). We are then told that Aaron spoke the words of the Lord
and "did the signs" and "the people believed" (Exod. 4:30,31). God
clearly gave to His prophets the power to perform miracles for the
purpose of helping them to convince their hearers that the message they spoke was from God and therefore was worthy of acceptance and faith.

This was also the purpose for which the miracles of Jesus were
performed. Toward the close of his Gospel the apostle John writes,
"Many other signs (or miracles) truly did Jesus in the presence of
His disciples, which are not written in this book; but these are
written, that ye might believe that Jesus is the Christ, the Son of

God, and that believing ye might have life through His name" (John 20:30,31).

Jesus Himself pointed to this purpose of His miracles when He said to the unbelieving Jews, "The works that I do in my Father's name, they bear witness of me. . . . Though ye believe not me, believe the works; that ye may know, and believe, that the Father is in Me, and I in Him" (John 10:25,38).

The apostle John expresses surprise and criticizes the Jewish people for not accepting this testimony of the miracles. He writes, "Though He had done so many miracles among them, yet they believed not on Him" (12:37). John's words clearly indicate that he expected a different result.

The result that John expected is illustrated by the case of Nicodemus. That leader of the Jews came to Jesus by night and said "Rabbi, we know that Thou art a teacher come from God; for no man can do these miracles that Thou doest, except God be with him" (John 3:2).

From all this it ought to be clear that in the Bible miracles are never viewed, as is so often the case in modern theology, as a hindrance to faith. They are intended by God, on the contrary, to serve as aids to faith.

But just as the miracles are done to substantiate the message of Jesus and of the apostles and prophets, so the message also helps to validate the miracle. Moses told the children of Israel that they should not listen to a miracle worker who would entice them away from the worship of the true God (Deut. 13:1-11). Thus miracles that accompany the teaching of doctrines at variance with God's Word are always suspect, and we may safely conclude that they are either fraudulent or performed with the aid of demonic powers, and should be described as witchcraft.

DEFINITIONS

It has been suggested that the old English word "wicca," from which the word witch is derived, is related to the word "wise." The English witch Sybil Leek says that witchcraft is the craft of the wise. This derivation is uncertain. We do know that witches were often called "cunning (knowing) women." One of the Hebrew words for practitioners of the occult is derived from the Hebrew word for "know" and means "the knowing ones." The magicians of Pharaoh are called "wise men" in Genesis 41:8.

It is agreed, however, that the word "wizard," which in the six-teenth century came to be used to denote a male witch, is derived from the word "wise," and it may be that just as a drunkard is a man who drinks more than he ought to, so a wizard is a man who knows more than he ought to, and apparently originally a wizard was one who produced Psi-Gamma phenomena.

The word "warlock," which is also a common term for a male witch, is an old English word for the devil. Literally, it means a "covenant-breaker," or a "covenant-liar." It later came to denote someone who made a pact with the devil and thus came into pos-session of magical powers.

The term "sorcerer" is the Anglicized form of a French word for magician which, in turn, is derived from the Latin word "*sors*," in the sense of "oracle" or "prophecy." It would seem, therefore, that originally it also must have had reference to Psi-Gamma phe-nomena.

Another word used to denote a wizard is "conjurer." To conjure originally meant "to swear together," "to enter into a conspiracy." Later conjuration came to denote the act of appealing to some sa-cred person or thing. From there it was an easy step to the mean-ing it has in witchcraft, namely to effect something supernatural by invocation or incantation.

The term "magic" is derived from the Persian word for "priest" or "wise man," and the word "magician," which today is largely used to denote a sleight of hand artist, was originally also a word for sorcerer or wizard. It is interesting to note, however, that the Greek author Heraclitus used it as a synonym for an imposter or a charlatan. He evidently had a very modern doubt about the super-natural.

Of special interest is the Greek word for witchcraft, "*pharma-keia*," from which our word "pharmacy" is derived. Drugs have from ancient times been associated with the practice of witch-craft. They were used and are used today to induce trance states, to cure diseases and to inflict suffering and death. Sybil Leek, for example, speaks of a fungus called the "Calendar of Death" which is tasteless and when fed to a guest causes a fatal illness of the in-testines in exactly eighty-four days, leaving no traces of its use. Whether this is true or not, it is typical of the sort of thing asso-ciated with the use of drugs in witchcraft. Much of the knowledge that made the witch a "wise" or "cunning" woman was and still seems to be connected with such drug use. It is not accidental that witchcraft even now seems to be closely associated with the drug culture in our time.

TYPES OF MAGIC

Magic has been defined as "a divinely forbidden art of bringing about results beyond human power by recourse to superhuman spirit agencies."[1] That definition probably needs to be modified so that it reads instead, "Magic is the divinely forbidden art of attempting to bring about results beyond human power by recourse to superhuman spirit agencies."

In the various forms of magic we ought to recognize the devil's aping of the miracles of God. In this area, too, as in the question of divination, unbelief sees no qualitative difference between miracle and magic, and it must be conceded that from the outside they often appear to be identical. We may not be able to say exactly how the magicians of Pharaoh produced snakes, but as far as outward form is concerned they performed an act that seems to be identical, at least up to a certain point, to the miracle of Moses. Yet Christians believe that there is a great difference between the two. Moses acted at the command of God. The magicians acted in opposition to God. The miracles were done to promote faith. The magic was done to hinder obedience to God. This is the test by which magic can be recognized for what it is, according to Deut. 13:1-5, where Moses says that miracle workers who encourage men to follow other gods are to be executed, just as a witch was not to be permitted to live (Exod. 22:18). We may define a miracle as a supernatural event performed with the help of God and at the command of God, whereas magic and witchcraft, if they are genuine, deal with supernatural events done with the help of the devil or his angels.

Much confusion exists in the area of the distinction between magic and miracle. A former Jesuit now teaching philosophy at a university, writing under the pen name of David Farren, says, "As a Catholic student and then as a Jesuit seminarian, I lived in the environment of magic and never realized it. *Magic* was not even in our vocabulary: we had the sacraments (like the Eucharist) and the sacramentals (like holy water), all of which conferred grace *ex opere operato;* non-Christians had superstitions."[2] His words demonstrate how easily confusion can be created between magic and the mysteries of the Christian faith.

It is not difficult to understand why an apostate Catholic should make such an observation since the sacramentals of Roman Catholicism are often little more than magical charms, but it is a little more surprising to discover that John Stevens Kerr, in a book published by Fortress Press, creates the same kind of confusion when he defines magic as "the art of manipulating the course of nature by supernatural means" and goes on to say that praying to God to avert a disaster or to bring rain is, "technically . . . as much a magical act as the Roman *haruspices* sacrificing a pigeon to the gods for the safe return of a general from battle with the barbarians."[3] This is surely a point of view against which Christian people must be warned in these days of the repopularization of magic and witchcraft.

Magicians and witches distinguish between "black magic" or "goety" (from a Greek word for sorcery, *goeteia*) and "white magic" or "theurgy" (from another Greek word for sorcery, *theurgeia*). The two Greek words in themselves actually seem to point to the difference between magic and miracle. The word "theurgy" literally means "the working of God," and it implies that the supernatural event is brought about with God's help. While the original meaning of "goety" is not completely clear, yet the word seems to indicate that there is some evil power behind the supernatural event.

Black magic involves calling upon the devil or evil spirits and is used to harm others or for purely selfish ends. Most witches claim to employ "white magic" in which the invocation is directed either to the Triune God or to spirits or gods classified as benign. Sybil Leek, for example, denounces black magicians and insists that all good witches believe in a supreme being. Yet she speaks of "incantations invoking the help of the Lords of the Watchtowers."[4] She distinguishes between "witchcraft" and "black magic." The first she says is a "religion" and the second "a debased art."[5] She claims to use her powers only for good. Yet she implies that it would be perfectly proper to murder anyone who would dare to reveal the secrets of the craft.[6] She relates in her *Diary of a Witch* how she once threatened to use "reverse tactics" (her term for what under all the rules ought to be called "black magic") on a black magician who came to her for help. When he objected that this was contrary to her principles, she replied "that evil may be justified if it is for the greater good of the whole."[7] She also says that in the practice of witchcraft all "sympathy, pity, affection, dislike . . . have to be put aside."[8] It is rather obvious that the differentiation between black and white magic is completely meaningless from a Christian point of view, and a Bible-believing Christian will be especially horrified at the use of the name of the Trinity or the name of Jesus in the incantations of magic. One of the members of my first congregation once told me of how she was cured of malaria by scattering a handful of barley in a circle around herself at the crossroads at midnight while reciting an incantation that began with the words,

> "Ich streue diesen Samen
> In meines Jesu Namen"
> (I scatter this seed
> In the name of my Jesus).

This is surely an open misuse of God's name which deserves the name "black magic" even though it has a show of Christian piety. Unger says that "white magic" is only "black magic in pious masquerade."[9]

Some writers speak of a third type of magic, which is variously named neutral magic or impersonal magic. In this type no personal beings, either "good" or bad, are invoked. At times such magic is almost pure superstition which in itself may not involve the misuse of God's name. For that reason it may be very difficult to demonstrate its sinfulness. People who believe that alfalfa tea can cure a case of nerves may have as little justification for their faith as a man who believes that warts can be cured by touching them with a round stone by the light of the full moon. Kurt Koch does not agree with this judgment. He says,

> My counselling work continually supplies evidence to the effect that magic in any form is the work of the devil, whether it sails under a black, white, or neutral flag.[10]

It is to be questioned whether "neutral magic" should be called magic at all. It may be nothing more than ignorance. The "science" of one age may well be the "neutral magic" of another. A Christian believer of centuries past who went to a surgeon to be cured of his illness by the drawing of a pint of blood from his veins and who did so with a prayer that God in His mercy might bless the hand of the surgeon may well have been acting in childlike faith. He was not calling upon evil spirits for supernatural aid. He was not placing his faith in a false object of worship. His confidence in the surgeon and his methods was undoubtedly mistaken, but while we might well label it superstition, it would occur to few people that we are here dealing with magic.

In the same way, the man who uses round stones to cure warts may in his ignorance of natural law believe that God in His wisdom has endowed round stones with such healing powers. There are people who believe that copper bracelets have a natural power to ward off arthritis and rheumatism. Who can prove that they are entirely mistaken?

If, on the other hand, the round stones or the copper bracelets would be used in connection with an invocation to a saint or some evil spirit, or if their efficacy were believed to depend on some magic incantation spoken over them by a person with supernatural powers, their use would certainly need to be classified as magic, either white or black.

Magic is also classified according to the type of magical act employed. "Sympathetic magic" works with analogy. The familiar voodoo practice of sticking pins into dolls to cause pain and even death is one example of this kind of magic.

When Jacob peeled strips of bark from twigs, so that the cattle at the watering troughs saw twigs with white streaks in them, in order to produce offspring that would show such striped markings, he was using what would by many people be called, and is called, sympathetic magic. What should be our reaction to such remarks? My hair has a tendency to stand up at the back of my neck when I read such things in the commentaries. Yet we know that some of the great heroes of faith were guilty of many sins. We know also that God can use the sins of men for His own purposes without approving of the sin itself, and therefore we ought to be careful not to defend Jacob absolutely against such charges, nor, on the other hand, ought we without question to accept those charges as justified. There is nothing in the text to indicate that Jacob used the name of God in vain nor that he called upon infernal spirits in practicing what could be called an act of superstition. Nor does the text in any way recommend that such methods be used by us. Nor does it promise that it will ever work again as it did in Jacob's case. While I would be rather reluctant to call it magic at all, yet I do not believe that this ought ever to become a doctrinal issue among Christians. Perhaps in the story of Jacob we have another illustration of Luther's remark that it will not do to construct articles of faith from the words and works of the fathers. Certainly no one ought ever to say that the Bible teaches that we can produce striped cattle by laying striped twigs in the watering troughs where they come to drink.

It may have been generally believed in those days, as it was believed for many centuries, that what was seen by a human or animal mother prior to the birth of her offspring could have a prenatal effect on that offspring. Jacob may have in that belief placed the peeled twigs before the cattle of Laban when they came to drink. He may even have done so with a prayer to the Lord that He would bless his efforts, and God may have used these means to give Jacob what he desired.

According to the teaching of the Bible nothing in the natural world has independent power, but that natural law is only God's ordinary way of dealing through and in nature and that whatever powers reside in natural means are placed there by God. Aspirin cures headaches, not because of some independent virtue, but because in His creation God endowed certain chemical elements with special healing powers. God still to this day works in and through these means, so that a man can say that God cured his headache, or the doctor cured his headache, or aspirin cured his headache without contradicting himself in the least. These are not exclusive but complementary statements. God can at times use unusual means to produce the desired results. Jesus' use of mud and the waters of the pool of Siloam to cure blindness (John 9:1-7) is an example of the use of means that in the ordinary course of nature have no such power. The peeled twigs of Jacob may be another such example.

In one place Luther says that when Eve believed that her eldest son was the promised Savior her faith was correct but she was mistaken in the person. In a similar way we may say that Jacob's faith was correct in that he believed that God would and did reward him for his many years of faithful service to Laban. We know that he looked upon his many possessions as evidence of God's mercy and faithfulness (Gen. 32:10). It may therefore be possible that Jacob was mistaken about the means through which God would operate. The account seems itself to indicate that God in a dream revealed to Jacob a better way to produce the results which he desired (Gen. 31:10-12). It should be evident that the text does not in any way imply that Jacob was employing magic in his dealings with Laban. At best it might be an example of "neutral magic," which, as we have seen, in certain cases hardly deserves to be called magic at all.

"Imitative magic" operates on the theory that like produces like. When pagan rain dancers imitate the falling of rain by the motions of their bodies together with the ritual chant or incantation, this imitative action, in theory, will produce rain. "Contagion magic" works with things that have been in contact with the person acted on in order to produce either a beneficial or harmful effect. For this reason people who consult witches are often asked to bring some object which has been worn by the person who is to be harmed or helped. "Contagion magic" is very similar to psychometric divination.

HOW WITCHES ARE MADE

A great deal has been written about the way in which a person becomes a witch or a wizard. It seems rather evident that most of the Protestant writers on the subject have done a great deal of plowing with Kurt Koch's heifer, for repeatedly one finds a repetition of his remark that most often such powers of witchcraft are hereditary and can be traced back over three or four generations in one family.[11] Sybil Leek, however, claims that her family has a tradition of witchcraft that can be traced back on her mother's side to 1134 A.D. David Farren, a former Jesuit seminarian, whose interest in witchcraft stems from his marriage to a "witch," says that his wife is descended from a line of thirteen generations of witches.[12] Women who have acquired their supernatural powers by heredity are called "genetic witches" by Farren.

Farren tells the story of how his wife became a witch. From the age of five her mother and grandmother instructed her in herbs and spells. At the age of eleven she was amusing herself with a Ouija board when she suddenly began to hear voices that told her she would not need to use the board anymore since she would hear the answers. The voices identified themselves as "the voices of God." She was committed to a mental hospital, diagnosed as an incurable schizophrenic. After two months in the hospital she had a vision telling her that if she did not want to hear the voices, which she was hearing constantly, she would not hear them. She recovered very quickly from that point on, much to the amazement of the doctors. But, according to Farren, (and it might be remembered that this man is a former Jesuit seminarian and a university professor of philosophy) she also from that time on had powers, which, if Farren describes them correctly, we could only classify as supernatural. Farren's description would seem to indicate also that it is sometimes impossible to distinguish clearly between witchcraft and possession by the devil.

Kurt Koch speaks of two ways in which the powers of witchcraft are passed down from one generation to the next. The first is by genetic inheritance and the second by what he calls "succession." By this, he says, "we mean the custom of a person on his deathbed actually bestowing the magical powers upon the eldest son or daughter in order to die peacefully." Koch says that at times the children do not want the powers, in which case the witch "may cry out for weeks on his deathbed for someone to relieve him of his magical powers."[13] The Spanish scholar Baroja says that among the Basques magical powers are transferred by accepting certain objects, often a pincushion or a needle case, from a witch, or by the touch of a witch on her deathbed.[14] It would appear, however, that, to a certain extent at least, the passing on of occult powers either by genetic inheritance or by deathbed transfer is often accompanied by instruction in the art. Both Sybil Leek and David Farren have much to say about such teaching.

Another method by which magical powers are supposedly transferred is by the laying on of hands. In this connection Kurt Koch speaks of a young man who did not have the gift of dowsing for water but who acquired it when a dowser held his hands while he held the stick.[15] Apparently Koch believes that this is not dowsing on a purely "physical level," of which he speaks in one of his later books,[16] for he says that after acquiring the gift the young man's love for the Word of God declined.

In regard to this type of occult transference, Merrill Unger writes,

> Sometimes magical powers are transferred by the occult ceremony of laying on of hands. . . . The history of occult practice often relates how one or more magicians, particularly those adept in black (devil) magic, impart gifts of healing or clairvoyant and mediumistic abilities by placing their hands upon the head of a per-

son desiring them and uttering magic charms and incantations.[17]

Simon Magus of Samaria apparently believed in such a transference of occult powers (Acts 8:18). This is an occult phenomenon that surely ought not to be left entirely out of consideration when we evaluate the modern charismatic movement with its practice of the laying on of hands. There may be a far closer connection than we sometimes realize between the revival of magic and witchcraft in our time and the rise of the Pentecostal movement.

While practitioners of witchcraft often speak of inheritance and transference as the way to the possession of magic powers, (Sybil Leek, for example, says that "most of the leading witches in the present era have a family tradition of witchcraft behind them,"[18] and Baroja says that "*all*" (our emphasis) witches and "*all*" magicians in Scandinavia were descended from three specific ancestors.[19]) yet the practice of acquiring such powers by making a pact with the devil has been known since ancient times. Such agreements were and still are often put into writing and signed with the blood of the witch. Merrill Unger says of this way of coming into possession of occult powers,

> Such blood-bound occultists frequently become endowed with astonishing magic capabilities . . . This practice of satanic blood pacts is not a mere superstitious hangover from medieval witchcraft and hobgoblins. It is a well-known and fairly common practice today in various rural districts of Europe where magic literature has circulated for centuries and magical powers have passed from one generation to another.[20]

Kurt Koch also speaks of the acquisition of magical powers that come from reading occult literature and experimenting with occult practices on one's own. He gives few examples of this and the case is not well made. But it may still serve as a reminder to us that interest in the occult for the occult's sake or experimenting with such things is potentially dangerous. Also here we ought to flee every form of evil.

Baroja says that according to Basque tradition one can also become a witch by walking around a church three times.[21]

WITCHCRAFT AS A RELIGION

Some witches insist that witchcraft is a religion. The English anthropologist Margaret Murray claims that it is the original religion of man by which man sought to bring nature under his control. She calls it the "Old Religion" and one commonly finds this term in the literature. In using the term "Old Religion," witches often make the point that their worship antedates and therefore is superior to Christianity. Jeffrey Russell, a historian who has made a study of medieval witchcraft, says "the historian knows that there is no evidence for Margaret Murray's view that witchcraft is an ancient religion that has preserved a marvellous continuity to the present day."[22] Baroja also rejects the view that the worship of witchcraft dates from pre-historic times.[23] For us this question is not important. It is enough to know that witchcraft is heathenism pure and simple.

The gods generally worshipped in witchcraft include Hecate and Diana, the so-called "horned god," whom Christians have usually identified with the devil, the forces of nature conceived of as personal or impersonal, the devil himself, and many others.

In the worship of witchcraft special efforts are evidently made to ridicule and blaspheme the God of the Christians. It may well be true that some of the descriptions of this worship found in the records of the medieval church are exaggerated. Those descriptions are based on confessions extracted under torture. Jeffrey Russell, however, says that some of the confessions were made in the secular courts and that therefore "there are good reasons for not rejecting them as fraudulent."[24] Baroja gives such a report from the records of the inquisition which says,

> They all walked over a cross, spitting on it, scorning Christ and the Holy Trinity. Then they exposed their hinder parts to the sky and the heavens as a sign of their disregard of God, and after eating and drinking their fill, they all had sexual intercourse.[25]

Baroja himself says,

> In witchcraft, Christian symbols and values are always used in inverted form. Whereas in Christian ritual the blessing is given with the right hand, witches use the left hand when making their spells. . . . At the mere mention of the name of Jesus all spells lose their power.[26]

Baroja records a prayer used at such services which reads,

> Come infernal, terrestrial, and celestial Bombo, goddess

of the crossroads, guiding light, queen of the night, enemy of the sun, and friend and companion of the darkness, you who rejoice to hear the barking of dogs and to see the blood flow; you who wander among the tombs in the hours of darkness, thirsty for blood, and the terror of mortal men; Gorgo, Mormo, moon of a thousand forms, look favorably on my sacrifice.[27]

There are also persistent reports of the sacrifice of infants, and some time ago *The Milwaukee Journal* reported that a woman in a divorce trial testified that her husband wanted to sacrifice their child to the devil. More may be said of this in connection with Satanism.

Some of the confusion about the religion of witchcraft stems from the fact that the worship services are held in secret. Sybil Leek says that it is a pity that the ritual of the Golden Dawn and the Sabbath ceremony must remain secret,[28] yet she herself gives at least some of the details connected with her own initiation into a witches' coven. Among other things she says that she was bound and a knife was held close to her heart while the high priestess explained what becoming a witch would mean. After that, she says, she took the oath of fidelity to the religion of witchcraft and joined in the ritual dances and incantations.[29] She implies that terrible things would happen to anyone who would dare to reveal the secrets of the craft. Many writers state that sexual orgies are connected with these worship services, that the *Book of Shadows* or the *Sixth and Seventh Books of Moses* are read, and instruction in magic arts is given.

While there are accounts of gatherings of multitudes of witches in medieval literature, it seems to be generally agreed that a coven or congregation of witches consists of thirteen members, usually, a high priest or priestess, plus six men and six women. The word "coven" is said to be related to the word "covenant" and signifies a gathering of people who have assumed an obligation to each other, or a group of people gathered for religious purposes.

The covens meet from midnight to dawn on the witches' "sabbath." Michelet says that the word "sabbath" when used in this sense is a corruption of the name of an ancient festival in honor of Bacchus, called Sabasia,[30] but I found this derivation nowhere else. Baroja says that in the Basque country of Spain, Friday night is the appointed time of the sabbath meetings in memory of the day when Christ was crucified.[31] Others say that the sabbaths are held on the night of the full moon, at the beginning of each season, and on the night of Jan. 31, April 30, July 31, and Oct. 31. In connection with the sabbaths it might be mentioned that Sybil Leek writes, "One of the marvellous things about a Sabbath meeting is that it always leaves me completely exhilarated."[32] Those who are impressed by the claims of charismatics who speak of the exhilaration brought by the "baptism with the Spirit" might take note that not all feelings of joy are inspired by the Spirit of God.

There are evidently a great many witches and witches' covens active in our day. Edward Tiryakian of Duke University wrote in 1974, "In the past five years witchcraft has come to life again in the urban centers of the United States, a country where one might least expect it to happen."[33] William Petersen says there are 10,000 practicing witches in Germany and 30,000 in England. He quotes Sybil Leek as saying that there are 400 covens in the United States, more than two dozen of which are found in San Diego.[34] Not all witches are associated with covens, however. It is, therefore, a problem that we can not ignore, especially because the television networks persist in presenting witches as perfectly normal citizens of the community. A related problem (of which pastors ought to be aware) is that it is a subject that carries with it a great deal of fascination for many people, which could only be increased by an incorrect presentation of the subject.

MAGIC PRACTICES

The magic practices which are carried on by witches are many and varied.

Sleight of hand

At the beginning it should be said that in popular terminology a magician is a sleight-of-hand artist, whose slogan is "the hand is quicker than the eye." To call a practitioner of this art a "magician" is really a misnomer, and where no claims to supernatural powers are made and no magical incantations are employed the practice is pure entertainment and not to be condemned as a sin, whereas true magic is always a forbidden activity.

Hypnosis

Kurt Koch classifies what he calls the criminal use of hypnosis as a form of magic.[35] Most psychologists insist that no one under hypnosis can be forced to do what he considers to be wrong, but Koch disagrees. He cites a number of cases to demonstrate that the views of the psychologists in this area are incorrect. Psychologists, however, do warn against the use of hypnosis by amateurs who are not aware of the damage that they may do. Koch's view is that some types of hypnotism can not be condemned, but that it easily lends itself to magical abuse. A Christian ought always therefore to be very cautious in this area.

Astral Projection

Apparently a very common magical practice is what is today usually called "astral projection," and which is associated with the ancient belief that witches rode to the sabbath meetings on broom sticks. That there were people who really believed that they did such things is conceded by scientific investigations; but it is commonly held that the experience was a purely mental state usually induced by the use of drugs. Leaves of certain plants were boiled or smoked, drinks or ointments were concocted from them and they were used to induce sleep. Baroja says that "sleep induced in this way brought with it fantastic dreams,"[36] and "that it is these opiates, then, not flying brooms or animals, which carry the witch off into a world of fantasy and emotion."[37] He also tells of a scientist who used a recipe given to him by a sorcerer to prepare an ointment which produced such a reaction.[38] Carlos Castenada, an anthropology student at U.C.L.A., in his book *The Teachings of Don Juan,* describes similar experiences induced by drugs to which he was introduced by a Yaqui Indian medicine man.

John Charles Cooper, in his book *Religion in the Age of Aquarius,* (p. 135) records a young man's account of an LSD trip, in which he said,

> I began to melt down into a little puddle of wax on the floor. I could see bright, irridescent colors of smoke, and I could taste the music — like salt and pepper. Then I seeped under the door and floated down to the beach. There suddenly the clouds parted and I watched my soul leave my body and go up through the hole in the clouds — and there I met God. He took my soul to the planet where it will live when my body dies from life on this planet. Man, was it a beautiful place!

The young man was waiting to get out of jail so that he could take an overdose and go back to the planet God showed him.

Whether this is the whole story of astral projection remains to be proved. Sybil Leek claims that two teachers at the school she attended were prepared to swear that she was present in two classes during the same period and that it was "only a simple matter of astral projection."[39] Yet later in the same book she describes astral projection as an experience in which the spirit is released from the body,[40] which she says "can be extremely dangerous." This definition could hardly account for the body being in two places at the same time. David Farren in all seriousness tells of such an astral projection trip across the Atlantic Ocean made by his mother-in-law, who on this trip brought back from Scotland a piece of jewelry which she left around the neck of her sleeping daughter.[41] The Rosicrucian order claims to operate with similar powers.[42]

That the phenomenon of astral projection is not completely impossible is demonstrated by the example of the apostle Paul, who experienced something that bears a resemblance to what is called astral projection by magicians.

Paul speaks of a revelation from God in which he was "caught up to the third heaven" where he heard things which it is not lawful for a man to utter" (2 Cor. 12:1-4). While it is common to speak of such events as "out-of-the-body" experiences, Paul is not certain that they can be called by that name, for he says twice that he does not know whether this happened "in the body or out of the body."

It is, however, clear that Paul did not seek out such experiences, nor did he experiment with them. He was grateful to God for the experience but he never advocated that this sort of thing ought to be practiced. To produce such phenomena by invocations and incantations is most certainly prohibited by the divine injunctions against witchcraft, but where they arise spontaneously, as in Paul's case, they can only be judged by their context and the use to which they are put.

Metamorphosis

The persistent stories which are told of witches who changed themselves into animals are perhaps to be explained as purely imaginary occurrences. They may well be accounts of drug induced experiences. Already St. Augustine in the *City of God* expressed doubts about the reality of such events and explained the phenomenon as a trance state in which the subject imagined himself to be an animal.[43]

Invocations

A term that occurs persistently in the literature of witchcraft is "invocation." This is in reality a neutral term which denotes a type of prayer. To "invoke" means, literally, to "call upon." It is a prayer in which we call upon God to be present or to help.

Invocation in witchcraft is usually directed to false gods or even openly to the devil. As such it is idolatry and a sin against the first commandment.

There is another element in magic invocation that should not be overlooked. In so-called "white magic," especially in Europe, the invocation may be addressed to the Triune God or the Lord Jesus. However, associated with magic invocation is the idea that by the use of the proper words the person invoked can be compelled to be present or to render the assistance requested. Such invocation, even if directed to the true God, is a parody of true prayer and a vain use of God's name, forbidden by the second commandment. All true prayer proceeds from a heart which considers every answer to prayer as a gracious gift of God's love freely given, and any notion that we can somehow exercise control over God and bend Him to our will is blasphemous. While we may pray unconditionally when we know that what we ask for is something which we know God wants us to have, yet the spirit in which all true prayer is offered is that expressed in the words of Jesus, "Thy will be done."

Incantations, Charms, and Spells

More common magic practices involve the use of incantations and charms or spells. These are verses or magic formulas recited either by an individual witch or in unison at coven meetings, which are intended to produce a magical effect. The word "charm" is derived from the Latin word "carmen" (a "song") and the word "spell" is the old Saxon word for "tale" or "story." It is the same word that forms the second part of the word "gospel."

"White" charms are often introduced with the names of the Trinity while "black" charms invoke the aid of three devils. Magicians insist that the spell must be recited in a precise way, syllable by syllable or it will not work.

What was said about magical invocation is true also of incantations. Even though the words and phrases may in white magic appear to be pious, yet they are a misuse of God's name because the purpose of an incantation is to control God and to bend His will to that of the practitioner of magic or of those who use his or her services. In black magic the incantations are an attempt to control and to use the evil spirits for one's own ends and to enlist their aid, which in essence is worshiping at Satan's altar.

Often the reciting of the spell is accompanied by a magic action, such as blowing, stroking or spitting. The object to be affected is sometimes sprinkled with "Easter water," which is water taken from a pond at 12 p.m. on Easter night, or with the ashes of a burnt snake, toad, bat, or bone.[44]

There are many types of charms. For example, one magic recipe recommends as a cure for stomach trouble the drinking of holy water while reciting the names of the Trinity.[45] The *Sixth and Seventh Books of Moses* recommend boiling a piece of swine's flesh in the urine of a sick person. The boiled piece of meat is then fed to a dog, after which the dog is supposed to die while the ill person recovers. Walnut leaves inscribed with Bible verses which are eaten unread are used to cure disease. A fertility charm also recommended in the *Sixth and Seventh Books of Moses* consists in placing a woman's hair between two loaves of bread which are then fed to cattle while reciting the magic words.[46]

When Bible verses are used as charms this again is a misuse of God's name. The Bible is given to make us wise unto salvation, and the use of the words of Scripture to produce magical effects is a violation of the very nature of Scripture.

Charms, Amulets, Talismans, Fetishes

The word "charm" has acquired also another meaning. Through the use of incantations and spells it is believed that certain objects can be charged with magical powers which are able to cure or inflict disease, attract the opposite sex, improve crops, bring rain, defend against enemies or danger in general, or any one of a hundred desired effects. The object so charged or endued with special power is called a "charm."

Such charms are also called amulets, talismans, or fetishes.

They may be worn around the neck, buried in the basement of a house, hung on a tree or fence, or used in other similar ways. Sometimes the charm consists of a potion to be drunk or an ointment to be rubbed on the body. Here again the witch's knowledge of herbs and drugs is undoubtedly of great significance.

THE EFFECTIVENESS OF CHARMS

Charms are often very effective. Kurt Koch tells story after story to demonstrate this. It is also a well-documented fact that African witch doctors are able to cause death by pronouncing a curse against a man and leaving a sign of the curse on his doorstep. Scientists usually explain such happenings as cases of autosuggestion by saying that it is fear that kills the man who knows he has been cursed. The fulfillment of predictions of death by fortune-tellers is explained in the same way. Kurt Koch, however, holds that the charms or curses often work even when the person involved is ignorant of what has been done.

Why do they work? Practitioners of witchcraft often express their belief that witches can direct a psychic force toward the object to be affected. This force is especially effective if a group of witches gathered for a Sabbath direct their powers in concert with one another. Such ceremonies produce what is called a "cone of power," which can produce magical results. The midnight hour is especially suited for such efforts since the world and also the person to be affected are at midnight more relaxed and therefore more open to outside influence.

The various studies in parapsychology may indicate that there may be some truth in these claims, but this can hardly be the full explanation. Some of the effects that apparently are produced go far beyond anything demonstrated in the laboratory of J. B. Rhine. It is hard to resist the conclusion that the devil's power is actually brought to bear in many cases of magic. If half of the stories told in the books written by Kurt Koch are true, then there can hardly be any doubt that witchcraft is effective today through the enlistment of demonic powers. It should be mentioned that Koch himself says that we must be very careful not to jump to the conclusion that we are dealing with genuine occult phenomena.

David Farren tells a story which would also seem to substantiate this. He and his wife visited a magic booth at a fair near Los Angeles, where he saw a copper amulet with his wife's zodiac sign.

The man in the booth who claimed to be a warlock tried to sell him the amulet for his wife and kept reducing the price until he bought it. A few days later his wife got a phone call from the man even though he did not know her name and her phone number was unlisted. He invited her to become a member of a black magic group and put her into a trance over the phone. Even though many attempts were made to get rid of the amulet it kept reappearing under the most mysterious circumstances, and Farren's conclusion is "that witchcraft does involve something more than hallucinations which might be attributed to an overactive fantasy."[47]

HEALING MAGIC AND THE CHARISMATIC MOVEMENT

Of special interest and significance in view of the modern charismatic emphasis on healing is the area of magical healing. Sybil Leek, for example, claims that she has a "flair for healing."[48] She tells in some detail of a cure she claims to have effected at long distance on a man in Rotterdam whose doctors had given him three months to live. It is significant that she says that the process of healing someone through psychic power resulted in a severe strain on her own health.[49] This would tend to corroborate Kurt Koch's statement that in magical healing there is always a detrimental compensation in some other area.

We have surely all learned to be extremely skeptical about reports of miraculous healing, for all too often such reports can not bear the pressure of close investigation, as the examination of Kathryn Kuhlmann's healing "miracles" by Dr. William Nolen, for example, have clearly shown. And yet we must bear in mind that one demonstrated fraud does not prove that no such healings really take place. The evidence for the genuineness of some of the cures seems to be rather strong.

In this connection, it is interesting to note that Kurt Koch, who accepts charismatic healing, openly charges in one of his books that the healing ability of Oral Roberts is magical rather than charismatic.[50]

All things considered, there would seem to be enough evidence for magical healing to warrant the conclusion that being healed can hardly in itself serve as a good basis for believing that the Holy Ghost has been active or that the person healed is a believing Christian. Even if the healing were real, it would still not serve that purpose well.

In fact, there are many things in the popularization of magic in our time that remind us of the charismatic movement. The more we become at least open to the possibility that witchcraft and magic are not pure invention, the more aware we ought to be that it is imperative that we remember that the spirits can be tried only by God's Word, and while the miracles confirm the Word and are intended to be aids and not the hindrance to faith which modern theology so often considers them to be, yet the Word must also confirm the miracle. False doctrine ought always to alert us that a false spirit is at work, and a charismatic emphasis which in any way detracts from the Word is always a work of the devil. When charismatics say that after they had been baptized with the Spirit, there was no more need to quote Bible passages, as one Lutheran charismatic puts it,[51] the spirit that motivates them is all too clearly revealed.

Kurt Koch, as we have said, is sympathetic toward the charismatic movement and defends it. Yet even he cites examples to demonstrate the danger that may accompany such phenomena. He tells of eighteen missionaries in Japan who were overjoyed when they received the gift of glossolalia at a pastors' retreat. Within a very short time, however, fifteen of the eighteen dropped out of mission work, one died, and the two others continued their mission work only after renouncing their charismatic experience.[52] He speaks of a school in France where about a dozen students became involved with charismatic activities while the rest of the student body rejected the movement. Sometime later all of the affected students had given up living as Christians while all the rest were still active.[53]

It is impossible for human beings to look at apparently supernatural or paranormal events and identify the spirit behind the event except for the context in which the event occurs, and the most important feature in that context is the Word of God. Where false doctrine accompanies the so-called miracle, the spirit behind the miracle is always suspect.

As far as magic and witchcraft themselves are concerned, both foes and friends agree that they can be extremely dangerous. On that account alone, all men ought to avoid it. Human reason itself would seem to indicate that it is a mistake to take laws against witchcraft from the statute books. But whether they are on the statute books or not, God's people will know that God wants them to have no traffic with any kind of witchcraft. He made His will clear when He told His people under the old covenant, "Thou shalt not suffer a witch to live (Exod. 22:18)."

THE SINFULNESS OF WITCHCRAFT

The practice of witchcraft and sorcery is forbidden in clear terms in the Holy Scriptures. As has been noted, under the Old Testament civil law, withcraft was punishable by death. In the Bible witchcraft is often classified with idolatry, fornication and murder. It is spoken of as one of the sins for which the northern kingdom of Israel was destroyed (2 Kings 17:17) and for which Babylon fell (Nah. 3:4). St. Paul speaks of it as one of the sins of the flesh which exclude men from the kingdom of God (Gal. 5:20) and in the visions of Revelation the apostle John sees witches and sorcerers burning in the lake of fire (Rev. 21:8, 22:15).

The Bible also speaks of the folly and the helplessness of witchcraft before the power of God. The magicians of Pharaoh eventually stood helpless before Moses and Aaron (Exod. 8:18,19) and finally were incapacitated by the boils during the time of the sixth plague (Exod. 9:11). The magicians of Nebuchadnezzar declared that what Nebuchadnezzar asked of them was impossible, yet what they considered impossible was done by Daniel (Dan. 2:1-49). In the New Testament Simon the magician and Elymas the sorcerer were helpless before the apostles (Acts 8:9-24; 13:6-11). Christians therefore have nothing to fear from practitioners of magic.

Christians also ought to recognize that witchcraft is no proper area for entertainment or idle curiosity. It ought to be as abominable to them as murder and fornication and idolatry. When the people of Ephesus were converted to the Christian faith they burned their books of magic (Acts 19:19), thus signifying a complete break with such practices. In that they set a good example for all modern Christians.

SOURCES
Chapter II

1. Merrill Unger, *Demons in the World Today*, Wheaton, Ill., Tyndale Press, 1971, p. 76.
2. David Farren, *The Return of Magic*, New York, Harper and Row, 1972, p. 83.
3. John Stevens Kerr, *The Mystery and Magic of the Occult*, Philadelphia Fortress Press, 1971, p. 70.
4. Sybil Leek, *Diary of a Witch*, New York, Signet Books, 1968, p. 61.
5. Ibid., p. 11.
6. Ibid., pp. 62f.
7. Ibid., p. 117.
8. Ibid., p. 51.
9. Merrill Unger, op. cit., p. 85.
10. Kurt Koch, *Between Christ and Satan*, p.77.
11. Ibid., p. 62.
12. Op. cit., p. 27.
13. Op. cit., pp. 62f.
14. Baroja, op. cit., pp. 231f., cp. also p. 133.
15. *Between Christ and Satan*, p. 65.
16. *Christian Counselling and Occultism*, p. 104.
17. Op. cit., p. 82.
18. Op. cit., p. 17.
19. Baroja, p. 47.
20. Op. cit., p. 82.
21. Op. cit., p. 231.
22. Jeffrey B. Russell, "Medieval Witchcraft and Medieval Heresy" in Edward A. Tiryakian, *On the Margin of the Visible*, New York, John Wiley and Sons, 1974, p. 180.
23. Baroja, op. cit., p. 243.
24. Jeffrey Russell, op. cit., p. 187f.
25. Baroja, op. cit., p. 91.
26. Ibid., p. 148.
27. Baroja, op. cit., p. 30.
28. *Diary of a Witch*, p. 202.
29. Ibid., pp. 61f.
30. Michelet, op. cit., p. XIV.
31. Baroja, op. cit., p. 147.
32. Sybil Leek, op. cit., p. 129.
33. Tiryakian, op. cit., p. 178.
34. *Those Curious New Cults*, p. 76.
35. *Between Christ and Satan*, pp. 65ff.
36. Baroja, op. cit., p. 254.
37. Ibid., p. 255.

38. Ibid., p. 205.
39. Sybil Leek, op. cit., p. 42.
40. Ibid., p. 155.
41. David Farren, op. cit., p. 36.
42. Max Heindel, "The Order of Rosicrucians" in Edward A. Teryakian, op. cit., pp. 147-151.
43. *City of God*, XVIII, 18.
44. Kurt Koch, *Christian Counselling and Occultism*, Grand Rapids, Kregel, 1972, pp. 135ff.
45. Kurt Koch, *Between Christ and Satan*, p. 74.
46. Merrill Unger, op. cit., p. 91.
47. David Farren, op. cit., pp. 36f.
48. Sybil Leek, op. cit., p. 105.
49. Ibid., p. 108.
50. Kurt Koch, *Occult Bondage and Deliverance*, Grand Rapids, Kregel, no date given, p. 52.
51. Rodney Lensch, *My Personal Pentecost*, Kirkwood, Mo.: Impact Books, 1972, p. 20.
52. Kurt Koch, *Christian Counselling and Occultism*, pp. 9f.
53. Ibid., pp. 8f.

3

Spiritism

"And when they shall say unto you, Seek unto them that have familiar spirits, and unto wizards that peep, and that mutter: should not a people seek unto their God? for the living to the dead? To the law and to the testimony: if they speak not according to this word, it is because there is no light in them."   Isa. 8:19,20

Introduction:

While the Bible clearly forbids all divination and the practice of magic and witchcraft, it is sometimes difficult for us to define these areas so exactly that we can know with certainty just what is forbidden. We may, for example, not know where to draw the line between spontaneous telepathy and a sinful invasion of another person's mind, or between a harmless misunderstanding of some of the forces of nature and a sinful faith in occult practices.

When we come to the area of spiritism, however, no such doubt can exist. Every effort to contact the dead for any purpose is specifically forbidden by God.

SAUL AND THE WITCH OF ENDOR

The Bible gives us one detailed account of what would today be called a spiritualist seance. It is the story of Saul and the witch of Endor (1 Sam. 28:1-25). In modern terms the witch would be called a medium.

Saul and his kingdom were threatened by an invading Philistine army. Saul sought advice from the Lord. When God refused to give Saul advice through the priests or the prophets of Israel, Saul determined to find a woman "with a familiar spirit." Witches and wizards had gone underground during the reign of Saul, because in the early years of his reign Saul had carried out the biblical directive which commanded the execution of witches. The servants of Saul were, however, able to find such a woman at Endor, in northern Palestine. Saul went to Endor, disguising himself so that the woman would not recognize him.

The king asked the medium to put him into contact with Samuel, who had died shortly before this time. The account says that the witch "saw Samuel," and that she cried out, obviously in fear. Her fear may have been occasioned by the fact that she saw more than she expected to see, but the text only indicates that she was afraid because she knew with certainty that the disguised man visiting her was Saul. It is clear, therefore, that this woman had access to supernatural knowledge.

When the woman described the man whom she saw and whom Saul evidently could not see, Saul "perceived that it was Samuel." When Saul then asked for advice, "Samuel" castigated Saul for his sins and told the king that he had been rejected by God and that the kingdom had been given to David. The words echo previous messages that Samuel had delivered to Saul from the Lord. "Samuel" went on to predict the death of Saul and his sons, by saying, "Tomorrow shalt thou and thy sons be with me."

Commentators have debated the identity of "Samuel" in this story. Liberal commentators, of course, reject the story as being largely legendary, since they believe that the sort of thing described here is impossible. Some commentators who claim to accept the account as historically accurate believe that the witch was a fraud and that she only pretended to see and hear Samuel. Such a view can, however, hardly be squared with the plain words of the text.

The text clearly indicates that this woman did see something. Moreover, she clearly came into possession of knowledge that she ordinarily could not have. Besides, her predictions were accurately fulfilled. The clear words of the text indicate that her knowledge of secret things came from the spirit with whom she was in contact.

However, a question that has been fruitlessly debated by conservative commentators is whether that spirit was really Samuel or an evil angel pretending to be Samuel. Martin Luther, for example, said that it was an evil spirit that imitated Samuel in appearance and dress.[1] Many Lutheran commentators, following Luther, simply assume that it could not have been Samuel. It should be noted, however, that the arguments presented for that view are often not based on solid biblical grounds. It is said, for example, that God would not permit one of his saints to be summoned back to earth. Nowhere is this taught in the Bible. In fact, it would appear to be contradicted to some extent by the appearance of Moses and Elijah at the transfiguration. God sometimes permits things that we might not expect Him to permit.

Others hold that Samuel says that Saul had "disquieted" him, and that this would be an impossible statement for a departed saint in the bliss of eternity. However, the word translated "disquieted" in the AV is not quite that strong. It really only indicates that Saul's efforts had had some sort of effect on Samuel. Even the translation "disturb," used in many modern versions, is a little stronger than the Hebrew word, which literally means to "move."

It is also argued that since Saul evidently died as an unbeliever, it would have been impossible for Samuel to say that Saul and his sons would be with him by the next day, since Samuel was in heaven. But the words of Samuel are naturally understood to mean that Saul and his sons would be in the next world, generally called Sheol by the Jews, where all the dead are.

The arguments against identifying the spirit as the spirit of Samuel are therefore by no means conclusive. There is also not one word in the text to indicate that this was an evil spirit. The spirit is simply called Samuel throughout. Moreover, the language is the language of Samuel (cp. v. 17,18 with 1 Sam. 15:19,28). The message given to Saul has the ring of a message from the Lord's prophet. Besides, it must not be forgotten that all the details of the prophecy were fulfilled. This is always characteristic of a prediction that comes from God, according to Deuteronomy 18:22. If we read the text without preconceived notions of what is possible and not possible the conclusion seems forced upon us that God in His wise government of all things permitted the spirit of Samuel to be brought into contact with Saul by this wicked woman. However, we must not make an issue of this, for the devil is a clever deceiver who often tells the truth for his own purposes. It is not necessary for us to debate such questions. That it was a sinful act on Saul's part to attempt to gain hidden knowledge in this way and that it brought him nothing but grief is made crystal clear in the text.

THE BIBLICAL PROHIBITION

Spiritualists seek to find justification for their sinful practices in the Scriptures. The Old Testament prophets as well as Jesus are described as accomplished mediums. Time and again spiritists speak of the experience of Jesus and His disciples on the mount of the Transfiguration or of the first Pentecost as the greatest seance ever held. Such remarks serve only to demonstrate that spiritism is the devil's mimicry of inspiration.

However, even the most twisted exegesis can not escape the conclusion that when God through Moses forbade the children of Israel to tolerate in their midst any consulter with familiar spirits or any necromancer (Deut. 18:11), He clearly and decisively laid down a strict prohibition against the practices engaged in by modern spiritists, or spiritualists, as they prefer to call themselves.

It is, however, not completely clear exactly what is meant by a "familiar spirit." This is the AV's translation of the Hebrew word *OB* , concerning the exact meaning of which there is some doubt. Perhaps all that we can say is that it is obviously an intelligent spiritual being with which a "witch" can establish contact. The Greek translators understood those who have familiar spirits to be ventriloquists. This may be an indication of a fraudulent attempt at giving the impression of a message coming from a spirit, or it may also be a reference to a phenomenon that we shall meet again in our discussion of possession as well as in connection with mediumship. In such cases the possessed person or the medium very often speaks in a completely different voice.

There is however, no uncertainty about necromancers. The Hebrew words here are very explicit. They are people who go to the dead with their requests for information.

That consulting the dead is a rejection of God's revelation is made clear by the words of Isaiah,
> When they shall say unto you, Seek unto them that have familiar spirits, and unto wizards that peep, and that mutter: should not a people seek unto their God? for the living to the dead? To the law and to the testimony: if they speak not according to this word, it is because there is no light in them (Isa. 8:19,20).

MODERN SPIRITUALISM

The practice of necromancy, or consulting the dead, probably never completely died out, but for the most part it seems to have been practiced more or less in secret.

The rise of modern spiritualism is usually traced to Hydesville, New York, where in 1848 Margaretta and Catherine Fox supposedly contacted the spirit world. The story of the Fox sisters and the subsequent growth of spiritistic activity in America and Europe is too well-known to be repeated. That the dead or at least spirits were actually being contacted was accepted as fact by otherwise highly intelligent people. When professional magicians, however, demonstrated again and again that all the apparently supernatural phenomena could be reproduced by natural means, when they exposed one medium after another as frauds, and one of the Fox sisters confessed that the so-called spirit rappings were actually produced by snapping their toe joints, spiritism suffered what appeared to be a death-blow from which not even the repudiation of Margaretta Fox's confession could rescue the movement.

After the First World War, however, spiritism once more began to flourish and the church notices in the daily newspapers carried long columns devoted to spiritualist services and seances. Yet it seems to me as I look back to those days that even most Lutheran theologians, who would not have dreamed of denying the supernatural, were almost fully convinced that spiritualism was trickery and deception from beginning to end. That much, if not most, of the spiritistic phenomena should be characterized in this way is probably true. When I was a student at Concordia Seminary in St. Louis in the late thirties, we heard a lecture by a Lutheran undertaker who was also an amateur magician and whose hobby was exposing the fakery of spiritistic mediums. I remember him saying, "I bury those people and I know that they don't come back." Such an attitude, however, could hardly be viewed as being characteristic of either sound theology or solid science.

BISHOP JAMES PIKE

The renewed interest in spiritism in the second and third decades of this century again faded away from public attention until the Episcopal bishop James Pike became a convert. His acceptance of spiritism is another example of how easily the wise men of this world become fools. Pike had rejected the authority of the Bible and all the fundamentals of the Christian faith. It is especially worthy of note that at the time when he became interested in spiritism he had even given up his belief in an afterlife.

It was a strange series of events that convinced the bishop that the dead are able to communicate with the living. He and his last wife, Diane Kennedy, have told the story of those events in their book, *The Other Side*.[2]

The story begins with the suicide of Pike's son Jim on Feb. 4, 1966. At that time the bishop, together with his chaplain, David Barr, and his secretary, Maren Bergrud, was living in Cambridge, England. It should be noted that both Barr and Bergrud also did not believe in life after death.

A little over two weeks after his son's death Pike found two postcards that he had never seen before lying on the floor in front of the nightstand next to his bed. The cards were arranged in such a way that they formed an angle similar to that formed by the hands of a clock at twenty minutes after eight. He was reminded of Jim, who was in the habit of buying postcards which he often forgot to mail.

Two days later Maren Bergrud came to breakfast with part of her bangs cut off. She apparently did not know that this had happened until Pike and Barr called her attention to it. The same thing happened the next morning, and Pike remembered that Jim had told him once that he did not like Maren's bangs and that she ought to cut them off. On the third morning the bangs had completely disappeared and no trace of the missing hair could be found.

That day Pike, Barr, and Bergrud made a trip to London. When they returned the next day they found two books lying in the same spot where Pike had found the postcards, arranged in the same way as the cards had been. Two photos had disappeared from the wall of the bedroom. When Barr opened the closet door he found the whole left side of the closet in disarray, and in the heap of clothes on the floor he found the missing pictures, together with some postcards they had never seen. They then found a clock which had not been wound and which had been stopped at 12:15 but which now read 8:19, with the hands therefore at the same angle as the postcards and the books. The coroner's report had indicated that it was somewhere near eight o'clock English time that Jim had committed suicide in New York.

A number of other unusual events reminded Pike and his companions of Jim and persuaded them that Jim was trying to get in touch with his father. An Anglican clergyman, who was interested in the occult and whom Pike consulted, suggested that they try to contact Jim with an inverted wine glass on a smooth table on which the letters of the alphabet, cut out of paper, had been arranged. When this did not work out well, although the glass did move, it was decided to consult Mrs. Ena Twigg, a medium who had also been suggested by the Anglican clergyman. A seance with Mrs. Twigg was scheduled for March 2.

On March 1, a whole series of highly unusual events, similar to those that had occurred earlier, took place. The next day, at the seance, the bishop was convinced that his son spoke to him with the voice of Mrs. Twigg. Jim had a great deal to talk about. He said that he was in a place like hell, that he could not believe that God is a person and that he could not be a Christian. At one point Jim was interrupted by another spirit who claimed to be Paul Tillich and who told Pike not to worry about Jim because he and others would look after him.

At a second seance a few days later Pike, who was leaving for the United States shortly, asked Jim how he could get in touch with him in America. Mrs. Twigg, in a trance and in a voice that sounded like Jim's, spoke the words, "Spiritual Frontiers, Father Rauscher, priest of the church, in New Jersey." According to Pike's testimony, neither he nor Mrs. Twigg knew anything about Spiritual Frontiers or Father Rauscher.

At a church service in New York a few weeks later Pike met the Rev. Arthur Ford, who in the course of the conversation mentioned that he was connected with Spiritual Frontiers. Pike was surprised and asked if they had anything special in New Jersey. Ford told him that Father Rauscher, an Episcopalian priest who was associated with Spiritual Frontiers, lived there.

Pike says in his book that he talked to his son again in August and September of that same year in five different seances. Between the third and fourth session Maren Bergrud committed suicide.

The famous televised seance with Arthur Ford took place about a year later on September 3, 1967, and in the next year, after a number of other remarkable experiences, Pike's book, *The Other Side,* was published.

ARTHUR FORD

Arthur Ford was an ordained Disciples of Christ minister. He had a long involvement with spiritism and was a well-known medium. In his autobiography, *Nothing So Strange,* he tells how the spirit of Harry Houdini contacted him. Houdini, one of the most celebrated magicians of all time, had devoted many of his efforts to demonstrating that spiritism was a fraud. But before he died he promised his wife that he would get in touch with her after death if he could. They arranged a private code that would be used so that she could be sure that it was really he if he contacted her.

After Houdini died in 1926 his wife offered $10,000 to any medium who could communicate with her in the secret code. After two years, when all efforts to contact her husband had failed, she withdrew the offer. In 1929 Ford supposedly was able to establish contact between Houdini and his wife and the spirit of Houdini spoke with his wife in the code they had agreed on. The editor of the *Scientific American* was present at the seance and a transcript of the session was made. Mrs. Houdini later denied that the code had been broken and yet the evidence seems to contradict her later repudiation.[3]

EDGAR CAYCE (Pronounced "Casey")

During one of the seances arranged by Bishop Pike another celebrated medium, Edgar Cayce, the so-called "sleeping prophet," who had died in 1945, made his presence known and tried to persuade Maren Bergrud to become a healing medium.

Edgar Cayce was born in Kentucky in 1877. Kurt Koch's statement that occult powers tend to be inherited would seem to be borne out by the fact that Cayce's father could make a "broom dance" and had such an unusual attraction for snakes that they would follow him home from the fields.[4] At the age of six or seven Cayce began to have visions. At the age of 24 he deliberately entered into a trance state in which he prescribed medicine and treatment for his own voice problem. From 1901 until his death in 1945 he entered into trance thousands of times. From 1923 on his "readings" were recorded by stenographers. He was not conscious of what he said, and it is reported that he spoke at times in languages that he had never learned.[5] There is no doubt that he used complicated medical terms with which he was not familiar in his waking state. His early readings all were given in answer to requests for medical help. Both friend and foe agree that the medical readings are most remarkable.

In 1923 Cayce began to give "life readings." These were pronouncements made in the trance state in response to questions about religious matters. When Cayce, who was a Christian Sunday School teacher, heard what he had said in the first of these readings he himself denounced it as a work of the devil. But gradually he began to believe in the readings and gave up Biblical Christianity as a result.

In addition to answers to religious questions, Cayce also made many historical predictions. The life readings are as ridiculous as the medical readings are amazing. He predicted, for example, that China would become a Christian nation by 1968[6] and that a new land, the lost continent of Atlantis, would rise out of the ocean in 1968 or 1969.[7] Edmond Gruss says that his prognostications are a "catastrophe," while his medical readings are "impressive."[8] It would appear that in Cayce we have a typical trance medium without some of the usual features of spiritistic mediums. In fact, Cayce for a long time refused to try to communicate with the dead. Still in some of the readings, spirits who claimed to be those of dead people did supposedly speak and Cayce's opposition to consulting the dead seems to have been overcome.[9]

URI GELLER

Another man who apparently belongs to this class of people is the young Israeli "magician" Uri Geller. His story had been published by Andrija Puharich, a Roman Catholic doctor of medicine, evidently a brilliant man, but a man who begins to appear foolish by accepting the most inane statements made by alleged spirit voices as great revelations of truth.[10]

Uri Geller has been denounced as a clever trickster by many. Yet his extraordinary powers were tested under laboratory conditions at the Stanford Research Institute. All possible precautions against fraud were taken and all test results in which there was any possibility of cheating were disregarded. Even under such conditions Geller achieved results that go far beyond anything that has come out of the researches at Duke University. According to the Stanford experts the chances of achieving the results achieved by Geller are one in one trillion.

Geller belongs into the spiritist fold because, according to Puharich's account, in his presence tape recorders begin to run automatically and messages from spirit beings are allegedly recorded. Although Puharich is convinced the messages are important, Geller himself expressed the opinion that he and Puharich were dealing with a bunch of clowns, because of the inconsistency of the messages. The account given by Puharich is rather impressive, and if what he says is true, there can be no doubt that there are demonic forces involved. Some people may harbor the suspicion that Puharich lives on the brink of insanity, but even that would not explain everything he says. It is certain, however, that most people would be inclined to laugh out loud when they hear that Puharich says that all the tapes disappeared before or after transcripts were made of them. Puharich is a scientist and knows that this is the normal reaction. Yet he feels compelled to relate such things. He says in his book, "It was apparent to me that I could never try to convince another human being of my experiences."[11]

Geller has been attacked as a fraud by professional magicians. Even though Geller was tested at the Stanford Research Institute, he is generally reluctant to submit to scientific testing. This is viewed as evidence of conscious fraud on his part. Yet Andrija Puharich, who has told Geller's story in his book, *Uri*, is himself a scientist who took strict precautions against fraud and deception in his experiments with Geller. Geller's reason for refusing to be tested repeatedly is that he says that he can never be sure that his efforts at producing apparently paranormal results will be successful. He claims that he cannot do his "tricks" by his own powers. The spirits with whom Geller has contact, if they really exist, are evidently capricious and unreliable. But Geller's refusal to be tested should at least be evaluated in the light of his own explanation.

ARIGO'

Before he became involved with Uri Geller, Puharich had investigated the claims that were made for Arigo', the famous Brazilian healer, who was definitely a spiritist. Arigo' claimed that all his surgical skill came directly from the spirit of Adolph Fritz, a German doctor who died in 1918, but whose spirit was now continuing his medical practice in and through him. Arigo' is a healer of the Espiritista Church in Brazil. This is apparently not what we would call a Spiritist group but a Pentecostal denomination with branches in Brazil and the Philippine Islands.[12]

When Puharich watched Arigo' operate he was so amazed at what was happening that he suspected that he and the other observers might be hallucinating, so he asked Arigo' to operate on a growth he had on his elbow. Moving pictures were taken of the operation and afterwards Puharich was given the excised tumor, which had been regularly observed by another physician for seven years. The operation convinced Puharich that Arigo' was not a charlatan, and that he had extraordinary surgical skills.[13]

On the other hand, William Nolen, a Roman Catholic doctor of medicine, investigated similar healing "miracles" in the Espiritista Church of the Philippines and concluded that fraud was involved.[14] In the Philippines he found that medical instructions came through "speaking in tongues," but, aside from the terminology, his description of speaking in tongues could be used as a description of a spiritualist seance.[15] Nolen also submitted to an "operation" for the removal of a tumor, which he was shown very briefly before it was destroyed, and after the removal there was no trace of any incision. This experience is completely unlike that of Puharich who says that the scar of his operation remains to this day and the tumor is still in a bottle of alcohol.[16]

While it has been clearly demonstrated time and again that much of what passes as spiritistic activity is clever deception, yet there obviously remains an unexplained and inexplicable residue that can only be viewed as truly supernatural. A Christian who believes in miracles and inspiration will not find such a conclusion to be *a priori* untenable.

MOHAMMEDANISM

It may seem strange at this point to speak of what may at first appear to be a completely unrelated subject, namely, the origin of the Mohammedan Koran.

According to Islamic tradition, the story of the Koran begins one night when Mohammed had a vision of an angel and heard him speak words which the "prophet" was able later to reproduce verbatim. Mohammed was not convinced that what he had heard and seen was real. He was afraid that he was losing his mind. When he told his wife Khadija about the vision, she tried to persuade him that God was speaking to him. She tried to convince him by pointing out that he never had done anything wrong. Mohammed was not convinced, because he said that all his life he had abhorred men possessed by spirits. He went to the mountains to commit suicide, but there he had another vision by which he was persuaded. John B. Noss in his book *Man's Religions* writes,

> When it began to appear that the strange experiences, in which rhapsodies in Arabic flowed across his lips, would continue spontaneously, without his willing them, he came to believe that Allah was using him as his mouthpiece.[17]

When we remember Paul's statement that the worship of the heathen is addressed to devils, we may well be moved to ask whether Mohammedanism is in reality only the invention of an uneducated camel driver.

In this connection a remark made by God to Moses at the burning bush may be significant. The Lord told him that as a sign that He had really spoken to him the Israelites would come back to this same place on their way to the promised land. This is indeed a remarkable prophecy since it would mean a long and difficult and apparently completely unnecessary detour on the way to Palestine. But the words would seem to indicate that Moses, too, like Mohammed, might begin to doubt the reality of the vision. One thing, however, is noticeably different. The argument that Moses is a good man who had never done wrong is never used in an effort to demonstrate the genuineness of his experience at the burning bush. Instead, God gives Moses a remarkable prediction whose fulfillment is to reassure Moses that he had not been hallucinating when God appeared and spoke to him.

SPIRITISTIC PHENOMENA

The apparently supernatural phenomena connected with spiritualism are many and varied, as in the practice of magic, with which they could also be classified.

The Ouija Board

Probably one of the best known and most common spiritistic tools is the Ouija board, which was invented a little less than a century ago and is now marketed by Parker Bros. The Ouija board is at the present time outselling the popular game of Monopoly. This so-called toy, which also many Christians use as an amusement device, is, according to many observers, actually very dangerous. It consists of a smooth board on which are printed the letters of the alphabet, and the words, Yes, No, and Goodbye. The board takes its name from the word "yes" in French (oui) and in German (ja). A small three-legged pointer or "planchette" is used with the board. Two people sit at the board with their fingers lightly touching the planchette, which moves until it points to one of the words or to individual letters in order to spell out other words.

It may be true at times that the planchette moves because one or both of the operators are pushing it subconsciously and that some of the remarkable answers given can be explained by telepathy. But this can hardly be the whole story. One competent observer states that in one experiment with a Ouija board the answers were spelled out at high speed when the operators of the board had their eyes blindfolded. A board was used in which the letters could be moved. When the letters were shifted around the planchette moved more slowly but it continued to spell out messages correctly and gradually regained its speed.[18] Such experiences seem to indicate that there are at times other forces at work than the subconscious mind of the persons using the board. John Stafford Wright says that "even if that which emerges is the product of their own minds . . . experience shows that what emerges soon becomes a conglomeration of evil, even if it starts apparently harmlessly."[19] We have already noted that Mrs. David Farren began to hear voices while using the board. This is not at all a unique experience since the same thing has happened in other cases.[20] Its use has reportedly led to devil possession,[21] and not only theologians, but also psychiatrists and medical doctors and even spiritualists warn against its use.[22] The passive state of mind required for its successful employment is a typical prerequisite for the invasion of the mind by alien spirit powers.

Glass Moving

The ouija board is not necessary to practice this sort of spiritism, however. The same results can be obtained by placing a glass upside down on a smooth table with one's fingers resting on it lightly. It will be recalled that this was the method used by Bishop Pike in his first attempt to contact his son.

Similar devices have been used for many centuries and in many different countries. The divining rod and the pendulum have also been used to spell out words in this way.

Table Tipping

Another common practice sometimes played as a parlor game, but also used in avowed consulting of spirits, is table tipping. One or more people sit at a table with their fingers resting on the table top. The table is then asked to move in a certain way to indicate yes or no answers or to spell out words as the letters of the alphabet are recited. Sometimes the tipping is preceded by an open request to the spirits in the room to indicate by the tipping of the table what they wish to communicate. This practice even if only used for amusement can become very dangerous to both the mental and spiritual health of those who engage in it.

Automatic Writing

Many people also become involved in spiritism by the practice of automatic writing. The planchette which is used with a Ouija board originally had a pencil as its third leg and it was used to write out messages in the same way in which it is used today to spell out words.

But such a planchette is not necessary. People with mediumistic abilities can sit at a table with a pencil poised above a sheet of paper and when a passive mental attitude is assumed, the hand begins to move of its own accord and writes out a message. After such automatic writing has been practiced for a time, it may take place spontaneously even while the subject is carrying on a conversation which has nothing to do with what is being written.

Kurt Koch quotes a psychiatrist who says that such writing can have a strong morbid influence on those who practice it. He also quotes a psychologist who holds that it easily becomes compulsive. Koch tells of a lady who felt the urge to let her hand write automatically in a restaurant, and when she was told by her husband not to do it, her hand began rapping loudly on the table and so persistently that she was unable to stop it.[23] While such automatic writing may at the beginning be nothing more than autosuggestion, as some hold, it should be evident that it can easily become a device by which spirit influence can invade the material world directly.

Levitations

The Ouija board, glass moving, and table-tipping all involve touching the object to be moved. Parapsychologists have demonstrated that it is possible to cause physical objects to move by mental concentration alone. Such telekinetic movements, however, are usually very slight. Spiritists claim that even heavy objects are sometimes moved significant distances up and down or laterally as evidence of the presence of spirit forces. Many such phenomena, called levitations or telekinesis, have been demonstrated as being pure trickery and deception. When Annie Besant, the founder of Theosophy, died it was discovered that her home was filled with all kinds of machinery that could produce such effects, and even her followers wondered why the machinery was necessary since they said that she could produce the effects without the aid of such devices. On the other hand, it is probably true that also in levitation and telekinesis there is an unexplainable residue.

A combination of such independent movements and table tipping is allegedly produced by placing the fingertips under the table instead of on the table. In this way, it is claimed, heavy tables, as well as other objects, can be lifted as though they were almost completely weightless.

Materializations

A rarer phenomenon in spiritistic practice is materialization. In materialization a body or part of a body appears and often the visible "spirit" is heard to speak. Cases of materialization are highly suspect because they usually occur in the dark. The Lutheran undertaker of whom we spoke earlier demonstrated at an actual seance that the "spirit" floating over the heads of those sitting around a table was nothing more than a piece of luminous cheesecloth on a stick. But the Bible surely indicates that such visible manifestations are not *a priori* impossible.

Appearances of angels are recorded in both the Old and New Testaments. They appeared either in human (e.g. Gen. 18:2) or in animal form (e.g. 2 Kings 2:11; 6:17). The biblical record therefore testifies to the reality of what would be called "materialization" by spiritists. However, there is no clear indication that the evil angels have similar powers. Whether the devil appeared in visible form to Jesus during the temptation in the wilderness cannot be determined with absolute certainty. His appearance to Eve during the temptation in the garden in the form of a serpent does not seem to be a case of materialization but the use of one of God's creatures as an instrument of evil. There is in all of Scripture no clear example of a visible appearance of Satan.

It may be possible that reported sightings of UFO's are examples of such materializations. Yet it is surely the part of wisdom to maintain a healthy scepticism in regard to all such matters. Puharich in his book on Uri Geller speaks of manifestations, which would be called UFO's by many people, but which only he and Geller could see. Other people who were present saw nothing unusual. If they were true materializations and not just hallucinations, one would expect them to be visible to anyone in the vicinity.

The subject of spiritistic materialization is related also to the various reports of "ghost" appearances. While many such appearances obviously are the products of overactive imaginations or clever manipulation, yet it would appear that not all such appearances are fraudulent or due to self-deception. John Warwick Montgomery, a Lutheran scholar, says,

> Ghosts are most definitely real. At least, *some* ghosts are.... After the cases of humbug have been rigorously eliminated, the number of such ghost experiences relayed by unimpeachable witnesses is most impressive.[24]

Apports

Similar to materializations of spirits is the phenomenon called apports. Material objects are made to appear or disappear without any apparent cause. The mysterious disappearance of the Uri Geller tapes is an example of apports. According to Puharich, Geller also caused a steel ring, which Puharich himself had placed into a sealed box, to disappear. Six hours later, while several persons were watching the box, they heard the sound of something metallic falling inside the box. When it was opened the ring had reappeared. Puharich says, "This is the first time I had experienced an object vanishing where I was certain that there had been no deception involved."[25] The phenomenon becomes very common in Puharich's experience after that, and more and more difficult to believe, even though Puharich seems fully aware of the need for careful observation and for guarding against deception.

In the case of Bishop Pike the disappearance of Maren Bergrud's hair and the mysterious appearance of the postcards and the books and other objects are also manifestations of apports.

At least one writer suggests that the serpents of the magicians of Pharaoh were produced in this way. He says, "Demons were dispatched to the desert at lightning speed by the satanic powers working with these men, and exchanged serpents from the desert rocks for the priests' sticks."[26] He does not say where or from whom he learned that this was the case. But again, those who accept the biblical evidence will not consider this explanation impossible.

The Bible gives us evidence to demonstrate that apport phenomena are not impossible. The resurrection appearances of Jesus demonstrate that a true human body that can be touched and felt can pass through locked doors and walls. In the language of modern science fiction, it can dematerialize and rematerialize, although such language may be based on assumptions that are not in accord with reality.

Such phenomena, moreover, are not mentioned only in connection with the resurrection body of Jesus. Even before His death Jesus evidently disappeared before the very eyes of His enemies (John 8:59).

Nor are such events associated only with Jesus. In the account of the evangelist Philip and the Ethiopian eunuch we are told that after the eunuch had been baptized, "the Spirit of the Lord caught away Philip, that the eunuch saw him no more." It is difficult to read those words and to escape the conclusion that we are here dealing with something similar to what spiritists call "apports."

Similar events were evidently not unsuspected in the Old Testament. When the prophet Elijah told Ahab's servant Obadiah to tell the king that he was present, Obadiah expressed the fear that the Spirit of the Lord would carry Elijah away to where he could not be found (1 Kings 18:12). The language there is very similar to that found in the story of the Ethiopian eunuch, although it may denote nothing more than a superstitious expectation on Obadiah's part.

Such occurrences are rather rare in the biblical record, and we may assume that true cases of apports are rare today, if they ever really happen. Any attempt to make them happen by magical means or spiritistic mediumship would come under the condemnation of God. In themselves they are not necessarily evil, but the means employed may be forbidden.

Seances

The most typical feature of spiritism is the seance. The word is derived from a French word meaning "sitting" or "session." Seances begin with a time of quiet meditation. Usually they are held in darkness or in very dim light, although this is not always the case, as is sometimes asserted. Often some object in the room will move as an indication of the presence of a spirit or spirits. After that the medium will usually go into a trance in which contact will be made with a spirit guide. Some mediums do not go into the trance state to contact the spirits. In the early days of the movement the spirit guide usually was an Indian chief, but this is no longer the case. Arthur Ford's guide was a deceased French-Canadian named "Fletcher." These spirit guides are evidently what was meant by the old term "familiar spirit." Whether this is also what is meant by the Hebrew word *OB* is uncertain.

The spirit guide then introduces the various spirits, all of whom, at seances, at least, identify themselves as spirits of the dead. Often, as in the case of Bishop Pike and Paul Tillich, the spirits claim to be the spirits of famous men, but the observation is often made that they must have suffered severe brain damage in death because their remarks are usually very trivial and not at all in character. The spirits speak with the voice of the medium who may suddenly switch from the third to the first person as the spirit takes over completely. Usually, however, the medium's voice will be raised or lowered in pitch. This communication with the spirits continues until the end of the seance.

It is generally agreed by Christian students of spiritism that if spirits really speak at a seance they are not the spirits of the departed but evil spirits impersonating the dead.

THE DOCTRINES OF SPIRITISM

That the spirits that speak through spiritistic mediums are diabolical becomes evident when we examine their teachings. We have already noted that Edgar Cayce gave up his Christian faith as a result of the revelations that came through his voice while he was in trance. The doctrine that overshadows all others in the theology that Cayce learned from his trance readings was reincarnation. He even came to believe that Jesus was the thirtieth reincarnation of Adam. Many of those for whom he gave readings were, according to the revelations that came to him, reincarnations of relatives of the apostles and of the family of Jesus. His biblical proof for reincarnation he then found in the words of the Savior, "Ye must be born again."

Before he died Cayce founded the Association for Research and Enlightenment, a study center devoted to the study of over 15,000 of Cayce's readings. Out of that study center has come a book in which it is said,

> For almost twenty centuries the moral sense of the Western world has been blunted by a theology which teaches the vicarious atonement of sin through Christ, the Son of God.... All men and women are the sons of God.... Christ's giving of his life ... is no unique event in history.... To build these two statements, therefore — that Christ was the Son of God and that he died for man's salvation — into a dogma, and then to make salvation depend upon believing that dogma, has been the great psychological crime ... it places responsibility for salvation on something external to the self; it makes salvation dependent on belief in the divinity of another person rather than on self-transformation through belief in one's own intrinsic divinity.[27]

It becomes apparent also why the devil would want to help Cayce give accurate health readings when we hear one of the people who accepted his views on reincarnation say,

> If his subconscious was right, where the professional medicos' conscious was so wrong, why shouldn't this selfsame subconscious be equally accurate and the professional theologians equally wrong?[28]

Shakespeare was correct when he said that the instruments of darkness tell us truths and win us with honest trifles to betray us in deepest consequence.

This animosity toward Christ and the doctrine of vicarious atonement is characteristic of the theology of spiritism, even though it may sometimes be masked. Victor Ernest, a Christian pastor, who in his youth was deeply involved in spiritism, has in his book *I Talked with Spirits,* told the story of the last seance he attended. The spirit control, after taking over the voice of the medium, announced that he was ready to answer questions on theology. Ernest, who had by this time begun to study the Bible, asked the spirit if Jesus was the Son of God. When this question was answered affirmatively, Ernest asked whether Jesus was the Savior of the world, and again he received an affirmative answer. Ernest then asked his third question, "Do you believe that Jesus died on the cross and shed his blood for the remission of sins?" Instead of an answer to this question being given, according to Ernest,

> The medium, deep in a trance, was catapulted off his chair. He fell in the middle of the living room floor and lay groaning as if in deep pain. The turbulent sounds suggested spirits in a carnival of confusion.[29]

This same attitude toward the cross of Christ is also evident from the Spiritualist version of the hymn, "Just as I am." Two of its stanzas read,

> Just as I am without one plea,
> But that, O God, Thou madest me,
> And that my life is found in Thee,
> O God of love, I come, I come.
>
> Just as I am, Thou wilt receive,
> Though dogmas I may ne'er believe,
> Nor heights of holiness achieve,
> O God of love, I come, I come.[30]

This attitude also became evident in the seances in which Jim Pike supposedly spoke to his father. He urged the bishop to publish his book in which he attacked the fundamental doctrines of the Christian faith. He also said that in the spirit world the others talked about Jesus but as an example, not a Savior, and that man must cleanse himself in the next world as he becomes more and more enlightened. While this is not identical to Cayce's views on reincarnation, yet the way of salvation is the same. This is part and parcel of the basic fabric of Spiritualistic theology and denial of the vicarious atonement is a necessary corollary.

In all Spiritualistic theology we find the most blatant type of work righteousness. The National Spiritual Association of Churches has issued a "Declaration of Principles" which says,

1. We believe in Infinite Intelligence.
2. We believe that the phenomena of nature, both physical and spiritual, are the expressions of Infinite Intelligence.
3. We affirm that the correct understanding of such ex-

pression and living in accordance therewith, consti-
tutes true religion.

4. We affirm that the existence and personal identity of
the individual continue after the change called
death.

5. We affirm that the communication with the so-called
dead is a fact, scientifically proved by the phenomena of Spiritualism.

6. We believe that the highest morality is contained in
the Golden Rule: . . .

7. We affirm the moral responsibility of the individual,
and that he makes his own happiness or unhappi-
ness as he obeys or disobeys nature's physical and
spiritual laws.

8. We affirm that the doorway to reformation is never
closed against any human soul here or hereafter.

9. We affirm that the precept of prophecy contained in
the Bible is a divine attribute proven through mediumship.[31]

CONCLUSION

From such a declaration of principles it should be evident that it
is really not important for us to know whether a spiritistic medium
is a fraud or genuinely in touch with the spirit world, for in either
case, spiritism promotes a theology that denies the gospel in its
totality as well as being in itself a clear violation of the law of God.
Spiritism is the devil's substitute for God's inspiration, and it is
worthy of note that in one of Edgar Cayce's readings he said, "The
Spirit of Forces (God) speaks as often to men as He did in the
past."[32] No amount of curiosity ought to tempt us to experiment
with that sort of thing in any form, whether it be a Ouija board or
a parlor seance. The psychiatrists tell us that often mediumship is
a way to insanity. What is even worse is that teachings of spiritism
can lead only to eternal death.

SOURCES
Chapter III

1. From a sermon on Ex 7:3-21 (St. L. III, 793).

2. James Pike and Diane Kennedy, *The Other Side*, New York, Doubleday, 1968.

3. John Stevens Kerr, *The Mystery and Magic of the Occult*, Philadelphia, Fortress Press, pp. 94-96.

4. Edmond C. Gruss, *Cults and the Occult in the Age of Aquarius*, Grand Rapids, Baker, no date given, pp. 109ff.

5. Jess Stearn, *Edgar Cayce, the Sleeping Prophet*, New York, Doubleday Bantam Books, 1967, pp. 11, 105, 257.

6. Ibid., p. 89.

7. Ibid., p. 34.

8. Op. cit., p. 117.

9. Mary Ellen Carter, *My Life with Edgar Cayce*, New York, Harper and Row, 1972, p. 113.

10. Andrija Puharich, *Uri*, New York, Doubleday, 1974.

11. Ibid., p. 122.

12. William A. Nolen, *Healing: A Doctor in Search of a Miracle*, New York Random House, 1974, p. 152.

13. Puharich, op. cit., pp. 26ff.

14. Nolen, op. cit., pp. 139-231.

15. Ibid., p. 189.

16. Puharich, op. cit., p. 29.

17. John B. Noss, *Man's Religions*, New York, Macmillan, 1974, p. 514.

18. John Stafford Wright, *Christianity and the Occult*. Chicago: Moody Press, 1972, p. 71.

19. Ibid., p. 151.

20. Gruss, op. cit., p. 104.

21. Ibid., p. 103.

22. Ibid., p. 105.

23. *Christian Counselling and Occultism*, p. 51.

24. John Warwick Montgomery, *Principalities and Powers*. Minneapolis: Bethany Fellowship, 1973, p. 137.

25. Puharich, op. cit., p. 97.

26. H. A. Maxwell Whyte, *The Kiss of Satan*, Monroeville, Pa. Whitaker House, 1973, p. 52.

27. Peterson, op. cit., p. 55f. (Quoted from *Many Mansions* by Gina Cerminara).

28. Jess Stearn, op. cit., p. 247.

29. Victor H. Ernest, *I Talked with Spirits*, Wheaton, Ill., Tyndale House Publishers, 1970, p. 32.

30. Quoted in Peterson, op. cit., p. 64.

31. Quoted by Walker L. Knight, *The Weird World of the Occult*, Wheaton, Tyndale House, 1972, pp. 27,28.

32. Mary Ellen Carter, *My Years with Edgar Cayce*, New York, Harper and Row, 1972, p. 29.

4

Demonic Possession

"When a strong man armed keepeth his palace, his goods are in peace. But when a stronger than he shall come upon him, and overcome him, he taketh from him all his armor wherein he trusted, and divideth his spoils.　　　　　　　　　　　　Luke 11:21,22.

". . . out of whom went seven devils"　　　　　　　　　Luke 8:2.

It is strange that a world which appears in large measure to have lost its faith in God seems to be intent upon demonstrating the existence of the devil, and many people who have lost interest in the truths of God's revelation display a morbid curiosity in demonism. Thirty-five years ago, it seems to me, anyone who would seriously have suggested that there are today actual cases of devil possession would in most instances have been looked at askance as incurably superstitious. This was even characteristic of most Christians. Liberal Protestantism widely denied even the existence of a personal devil. One of the most noted theologians of that generation wrote,

> I maintain that to revive or perpetuate the demonology
> of the New Testament in the modern world is to incur
> the charge of obscurantism and superstition. The
> church should do all in her power to root it out, for it can
> only stultify her proclamation.[1]

The more conservative admitted that there were cases of devil possession in New Testament times but seriously questioned whether such things could still happen today.

But in the past decade we have seen a long list of novels and films dealing with the subject of devil possession and devil worship. *Rosemary's Baby, The Exorcist,* and the *Omen* are perhaps the best known. A serious scholarly study of possession and exorcism by the Jesuit professor Malachi Martin has been published by the Reader's Digest Press and our newspapers and newsmagazines from time to time carry articles dealing with the subject. My own impression is that none of these things could have happened a third of a century ago.

DEVIL POSSESSION IN THE BIBLE

No Bible-believing Christian can deny the possibility and the reality of demonic possession. The Bible tells us in clear and unmistakable terms that there were people possessed by devils who were cured by the Lord Jesus and by the apostles. To doubt the possibility of demonization is to doubt the authority of Scripture, and even the apostate priest David Farren says, "From a reconsideration of whether Jesus did 'drive out devils' to whether the Resurrection was an actual event is a very short step."[2]

In spite of the clear statements of Scripture, however, there have been many so-called Christian scholars who have denied that there is such a thing. They have attempted to explain the biblical language by saying that Jesus and the evangelists were children of their time. By the Jews of that unenlightened, prescientific age it was commonly held, so it is argued, that both physical and mental illnesses were caused by devils. If Jesus effected any cures, and even liberal critics will admit that He did, they were cases of psychosomatic illness which were cured by suggestion.

If it was so commonly believed that diseases were caused by devils we might ask why it is that the great majority of illnesses cured by Jesus are not ascribed to devil possession. Of the twenty-four healing miracles described in some detail in the four Gospels, only six (or seven if we include the woman in Luke 13:11) are designated as cases of devil possession. The Gospels, as we have already noted, also make a very clear distinction between disease and devil possession. Matthew, for example, says that they brought to Jesus "all sick people that were taken with divers diseases and torments and those which were possessed with devils" (Matt. 4:24).

Moreover, such a view could not be held by anyone who believes that the Bible is the verbally inspired and inerrant Word of God and accepts the deity, omniscience, and truthfulness of the Savior.

Closely related to this way of looking at the matter is the opinion of those who say that there is no such thing as devil possession, that Jesus knew that there was no such thing, but that He accommodated Himself to the views of the populace and went along with them in order to heal by suggestion those who believed themselves to be possessed. While such a view may seem to uphold the omniscience of the Savior, it is certainly an attack on His truthfulness and on the reliability of the inspired record, so that no Bible-believing Christian can hold such an opinion.

Historical-critical scholarship is inclined to view the stories of the healing of demoniacs as an outgrowth of the conviction of the early Christians that Jesus had come to destroy the works of the devil. Whether or not He really cast out devils is a subject of little concern to the critical scholars. The important lesson to remember, according to their view, is that in Jesus the forces of evil are overcome. The individual believer thus is left free to believe in the reality of demonic possession or not, as he chooses. In this way another obstacle to ecumenical togetherness is removed.

It is sometimes held that devil possession is just another name for mental illness. Aside from the fact that such a view also violates the clear statements of the Gospels, it should be pointed out that in only one, or at the most three cases, do we have any clear reference to what would appear to be beyond question mental aberration in the demoniac. The Gadarene demoniac displays some of the classic symptoms of a schizoid and paranoid personality, but it is to be questioned whether this would explain his superhuman strength. The demoniac boy whom Jesus healed after the transfiguration (Matt. 17:14; Mark 9:17; Luke 9:38) exhibits the symptoms of epilepsy which surely ought to be classified as at least partially a physical illness. Whether the shouting of the demoniac in the synagogue of Capernaum (Mark 1:23; Luke 4:33) is a mark of mental illness or not could be debated. In the case of the dumb demoniac (Matt. 9:32) and the dumb and blind demoniac (Matt. 12:22; Luke 11:14) nothing is said that would suggest any kind of mental illness. Only their physical affliction is mentioned. In the case of the daughter of the Syro-Phenician woman we are only told that she was "grieviously vexed by the devil" (Matt. 15:21; Mark 7:24), which does not tell us much about her symptoms. If the woman in Luke 13, who could not stand up straight, and of whom Jesus said that Satan had bound her for eighteen years (13:16), is included in the list of demoniacs, we have another case of what would appear to be a purely physical affliction brought on by the devil. Devil possession evidently can manifest itself in various ways.

When the biblical statements are taken at face value the only possible conclusion to which we can come is that at least in New Testament times people were possessed by devils and that Jesus and His disciples actually cast them out. On this conclusion there is no room for compromise.

There are no clear cases of devil possession described in the Old Testament, although the book of Samuel says of Saul, the first king of Israel, that the Spirit of the Lord departed from him and that "an evil spirit from the Lord troubled him" (1 Sam. 6:14). The uncontrollable rages to which Saul became subject may indicate that we are also here dealing with a case of devil possession.

A rather strange story concerning the influence of demons on the lives of men is found in the apocryphal book of Tobit. According to the book of Tobit, a wicked demon, called Asmodeus, killed any man who married Sarah, the daughter of Raguel. After seven men had been slain, Sarah was married to Tobias (the son of Tobit), who drove the evil demon away by burning the liver and heart of a fish which had been given to him by the angel Raphael, who then bound Asmodeus in Egypt so that he could not trouble the young couple. This, however, could hardly be viewed as an example of devil possession.

DEMON POSSESSION AND DIVINATION

In the book of Acts there is a story dealing with demon possession that may be of great significance in the evaluation of modern psychics who claim to be able to predict the future. When Paul came to Philippi he met a young slave girl who was "possessed with a spirit of divination" (Acts 16:16). The NIV says that she "had a spirit by which she predicted the future." By her fortune telling she made a great deal of money for her owners. She must therefore have acquired a reputation as a skilled fortune teller. She seems also to have had some supernatural knowledge of the nature of Paul's work, for she followed Paul through the streets of the city, crying, "These men are the servants of the most high God, which show unto us the way of salvation."

What is most significant, as applied to modern fortune telling, is that when Paul exorcised the spirit and commanded him to leave, the girl lost her ability to tell fortunes. If her practice of divination had been pure fraud, there is no reason why she could not have continued to earn money for her masters in this way. But even her masters knew "that the hope of their gains was gone" (Acts 16:19) when the girl was no longer possessed.

Writers who have investigated the occult often observe that the means used to predict the future or to gain other hidden knowledge, whether they be cards, crystal balls, rods and pendulums, or other means, all seem to work best when they are employed by people who have mediumistic abilities. In Biblical terms we would describe them as people who have "a spirit of divination."

It may, therefore, be true that many genuine psychics, whose guesses about the future or about hidden matters occasionally find remarkable fulfillment, may well belong to the class of demoniacs. Or, at least, they may be in actual touch with evil spirits who are sometimes in possession of information which enable them to make shrewd guesses about the future or to reveal matters which could not be known by natural means.

DEMONIC POSSESSION TODAY

Whether there is such a thing as devil possession today is at least subject to question. The question probably cannot be answered with absolute finality without a revelation from God, since we are here dealing with things which are beyond the measuring capacity of scientific instruments. However, I must say that, for myself, I am convinced of the occurrence of the phenomenon in the modern world.

However, it is probably not as common as the present spate of literature and the surge of interest in the subject might seem to imply. One of the exorcists in Malachi Martin's book says that "out of every hundred claimants there might be one genuine case."[3] A French Roman Catholic expert on possession, Henri Gesland, reported that from 1968 to 1974 he was consulted in 3,000 cases of suspected possession, and that he believes that out of the 3,000 there were only four that he could consider to be genuine. Such restrained estimates would surely seem to indicate, however, that the evidence must finally overwhelmingly point to the fact that sometimes human beings actually do become demonized.

In contrast to the questioning attitude of Gesland, Martin quotes the German psychologist, T.K. Oesterreich as saying "that 'possession has been an extremely common phenomenon, cases of which abound in the history of religion.' "[4] This, however, gives a wrong impression because Oesterreich, who wrote a book on possession (*Die Bessessenheit*) in the 1920's, did not believe that actual demons took possession of human beings. He considered possessed people to be neurotics and the supposed demons that possessed them to be nothing more than an aspect of their own personalities. Strictly speaking, therefore, in our terms we ought to say that Oesterreich himself does not believe that there are any demoniacs at all, but only many people who believe themselves or who are believed by others to be possessed of demons.

It is obvious that there are many neurotics who imagine themselves to be possessed. Michelet, for example, records the case of a nun in France who declared that she had three devils, one was a good-natured Catholic devil, the second was a bad devil, a freethinker and a Protestant, and the third was the demon of impurity. Michelet says that she forgot to mention the demon of jealousy.[5] In Baroja's study of witchcraft we are told that there was a proliferation of cases of possession in Spain in the late 1600's. He believes that it was provoked by "too much reading of books on witchcraft and demoniacal possession written by influential theologians."[6] We may be in danger of the same sort of thing today, for much of the modern interest in the occult is definitely unwholesome. One modern student of the occult, for example, quotes a Christian psychiatrist as saying that "much talking about demons can bring about all sorts of neurotic conditions."[7]

When Gesland accepts only four out of 3,000 alleged cases as genuine, it is clear that statistically speaking he agrees almost fully with Oesterreich, even if on the philosophical question of the possibility of true demonization they are poles apart. For this reason also the Roman Catholic Church insists that before any exorcism can be performed legitimately, the subject must first of all be examined by medical doctors and psychiatrists to weed all those who suffer from one sort of neurosis or another. Malachi Martin speaks of a neurological condition called "Tourette's syndrome," which manifests some of the typical symptoms of devil possession, such as "profanity, obscenity, grunts, animal noises, facial contortions," and which he considers to be a disease involving a chemical abnormality in the brain.[8] The disease yields to drug treatment. From that Martin concludes that it can not be possession. Whether this is a proper conclusion may be questioned, since there seems to be a widely held opinion that the onset of possession may be occasioned by drug use. If the use of certain drugs can make it easier for the devil to invade the personality, then it could conceivably also be true that the use of other drugs might inhibit the activity of demons.

While we must be on our guard against a naive and gullible attitude, it seems to me that the evidence presented to demonstrate that there is such a thing as devil possession today is so overwhelming that it is more difficult not to believe than to believe. Only someone who is predisposed to deny the existence of the supernatural would have a good logical premise on which to base his rejection of the evidence. On the other hand it also seems well established that much of what appears to some people to be demonization is neurotic imagination, which may be encouraged by leaving the impression that possession is a common occurrence.

CASES

In 1968 Kregel's publishing house reprinted a book dealing with the subject of demon possession which had first been printed in 1894. The author was John B. Nevius, a man who had served as a Presbyterian missionary in China for almost forty years. Nevius says in his book that when he first came to China in 1854 he brought with him "a strong conviction" that a belief in demons, and communication with spiritual beings, belongs exclusively to a barbarous and superstitious age, and at present can consist (coexist) only with mental weakness and want of culture."[9]

After about twenty years Nevius was convinced by his experiences that devil possession was rather common in China and that the coming of Christianity had a tendency to reduce the number of demoniacs in a region. He therefore wrote letters to other Christian missionaries asking them to supply him with information concerning possession in their area. In his book he cites many cases which were reported to him as a result of this letter, and he says that he consciously used only material for which he had the personal testimony of intelligent observers.

Even more striking is the evidence presented by Malachi Martin in his book *Hostage to the Devil*. Martin, as we have already noted, is a Jesuit professor. In *Hostage to the Devil* he tells the story of five exorcisms based on actual tape recordings made at the exorcism sessions. He writes,

> The following five cases are true. The lives of the people involved are told on the basis of extensive interviews

with all of the principals involved, with many of their friends and relatives, and with many others involved directly or indirectly in minor ways. All interviews have been independently checked for factual accuracy wherever possible. The exorcisms themselves are reproduced from the actual tapes made at the time and from the transcripts of those tapes.[10]

The first story he tells is that of Marianne K., a young Polish Catholic girl in New York who gradually slipped into an unbelievably depraved and immoral life. The facts as they are recorded by Martin are utterly revolting. As an example of her depravity we might only mention that she refused to see her parents, and when her mother left a food package at the door of Marianne's apartment, the girl sent her mother's gift back to her in a dripping and smelly package in which she had mixed excrement and urine with the food her mother had left.

Marianne had a married brother to whom she had been very close. When he came to New York, he went to visit her. On his mother's insistence he took with him a crucifix, which she wanted him to leave somewhere in the apartment. When Marianne left the room, he placed the crucifix under the mattress of her bed. According to Martin's account,

> No sooner had Marianne returned and sat on the edge of the bed than she turned white as chalk and fell rigidly to the floor, where she lay jerking her pelvis back and forth as though she were in great pain. In seconds the expression on her face had changed from dreamy to almost animal; she foamed at the mouth and bared her teeth in a grimace of pain and anger.[11]

In this state she was taken to her parents' home, where she remained for weeks in a comatose state, but when the parish priest came she had "terrifying fits of rage and violence." She was examined by doctors who could find nothing organically wrong. Almost unbelievably a psychiatrist "pronounced her normal within the definition of any psychological test."[12]

Marianne's parents finally asked the diocesan authorities for permission to have an exorcism performed. The exorcism lasted for nineteen hours before the demon was finally cast out and Marianne returned to normal. The record of the exorcism taken from the actual tape recordings made at the time is so coarse and so blasphemously diabolic as to be frightening. What struck me, however, as being of particular significance is the fact that the exorcist was a Hebrew scholar and the girl spoke to him in Hebrew during the course of the exorcism.[13] I wish Martin had investigated the question of whether she had ever come into contact with the Hebrew language in her college training.

The second case described by Martin is that of a priest, who had adopted a thoroughly naturalistic theology and who began to change the words of the liturgy under compulsion, so that instead of "This is My body," he would say instead "This is My tombstone." While the record as Martin gives it of this possessed priest does not contain the same kind of obsenity that is found in the case of Marianne K, yet when we are told that instead of "This is My blood" he would consecrate the wine with the words "This is My sexuality," we surely recognize this as a type of obscenity that is even more depraved than the mere spouting of four-letter words. He would baptize babies in the name of "the sky, the earth, and the water." Side by side with his service in the Catholic church he conducted another type of worship for a congregation in a rented apartment. In the regular worship service he found it almost impossible to make the sign of the cross, and finally once when he was saying mass he was catapulted away from the altar and thrown to the floor of the sanctuary. It was then that his superiors finally came to the conclusion that he was possessed. The priest who tried for two years to exorcise the devil became possessed himself for a time, and the case is particularly interesting because it illustrates how the dogma of evolution serves the devil's purpose.

The third of Martin's examples is that of a man who had gone through a sex change operation. At the first attempt at exorcism, the officiating priest was physically attacked by the demon and was hurled across the room and slammed against the wall. The account in some ways is reminiscent of the attack on the seven sons of Sceva recorded in the book of Acts (19:13-16). At the final exorcism session some weeks later, after the priest had recovered from the attack, an unbelieving psychiatrist was present. One of the witnesses later testified that the expression on the face of the psychiatrist changed from one of business as usual, to incredulity, to impatience, and finally to fear. The psychiatrist regained his composure and interfered in the exorcism with results that terrified the whole group present, especially the psychiatrist. It is also interesting to note that when the spirits finally left the possessed person, they said of the psychiatrist that the exorcist could not have him. They asserted, "We already have his soul. We claim him. He is ours. And you cannot do anything about that. We already have him. He is ours. We needn't fight for him."[14] Martin believes that the psychiatrist may have been a case of "total possession," for which there is no cure.

We can not, in the space available to us, discuss in any detail the two other cases described in Martin's book, but one of the cases might be mentioned because it differs markedly from the other four. It is a case of what Martin calls "familiarization." In familiarization, according to Martin, the physical violence, the stench, the social aberrations and moral degeneracy that is characteristic of other forms of possession are absent. The "familiar" seeks to live with the victim, but does not take over his personality. Martin says that the intelligence of familiars is very low, and that they are bound by rules and are in strict dependence on a "higher" intelligence. Nevertheless it is clear that they are evil, and in the case described, the familiar twice almost convinced the possessed person to commit suicide. At the same time, however, the victim, who was a radio announcer, received a great deal of help from his familiar who called himself "Uncle Ponto."

SYMPTOMS OF DEMONIZATION

The question of how demonization differs from mental illness is one that is very important. We have already noted that the hierarchical authorities of the Roman Church do not authorize exorcisms at the present time unless the candidate for exorcism has been pronounced psychologically normal by competent examiners. Martin tells of a young boy who was treated for epilepsy for a period of years and finally was sent to a hospital for treatment. After thorough examination he was declared nonepileptic and completely healthy, but when he returned home the "dreadful disturbance began all over again in a much more emphasized way." The attacks ceased only after the boy was exorcised by the same priest who exorcised Marianne K.[15]

In Kurt Koch's book *Occult Bondage and Deliverance,* the Christian psychiatrist, Alfred Lechler, discusses the distinction between disease and the demonic at some length (pp. 133-190). Dr. Lechler lists seven characteristics of devil possession. They are 1)a double voice, 2) clairvoyance 3) paroxyms 4) great bodily strength 5) resistance to divine things 6) exorcism during attacks 7) complete cure after expulsion (p. 256). Very similar symptoms are listed by other researchers. The Roman Catholic ritual of exorcisms lists four special symptoms that distinguish possession. They are 1) knowledge of languages not previously known, 2) knowledge of secret or remote things, 3) manifestations of unnatural strength, and 4) aversion toward God and the church.

It is striking to note as one reads the literature on the subject how the same themes occur again and again whether the background is Chinese or American, whether the author believes in the supernatural or not. The symptoms remain the same. T. K. Oesterreich, for example, says that the typical distinguishing marks of possession remain constant through the ages. He writes,

> The descriptions by the New Testament writers bear
> the stamp of truth, even if they should prove to be par-
> tially or even in every case unhistorical. They are typi-
> cal pictures of conditions correctly reproduced.[16]

Change in Personality

One of the symptoms that is regularly noted is that there is a complete change in the personality of the possessed person. In the early stages of possession this may seem to be a normal change. A young man or young woman, for example, may at first manifest nothing more than juvenile rebellion against authority, which may be viewed by many as a part of the maturation process.

The type of change that takes place varies greatly. Some may become ecstatic while others become morose and even suicidal. Between attacks the afflicted person may seem to be completely normal. Up to this point there is no special reason to suspect demonization.

Together with the change in personality there is often a pronounced change in facial expression. At one moment the eyes may be normal and the next a pleasant face will be replaced by a grimace that can only be described as diabolical. There may even be a rapid series of changes in appearance.

At the beginning, it seems, the invading spirit will usually pretend to be only another side of the patient's personality, but eventually the spirit will begin to speak of the possessed person as a distinct individual. Many times the spirit, though he is using the voice of the patient, will speak of himself in the first person, to other people in the room in the second person, but will use the third person when speaking of the one possessed. Often the plural of the first person is used. The use of the plural pronoun, indicating multiple possession, is familiar to Bible readers from the story of the Gadarene demoniac, who, in answer to Jesus' question, "What is your name?" answered, "My name is legion; for we are many" (Mark 5:9). The Bible also specifically says that "many devils were entered into him" (Luke 8:30).

Malachi Martin says that during an exorcism the spirit always makes a special effort to pretend to be the possessed person, but as this pretense begins to break down, the filth and violence increases, until finally, at what he calls the breakpoint, the spirit for the first time speaks of the possessed in the third person.

Unger believes that this use of the third person is one of the marks by which possession can be distinguished from insanity. He says that an insane person may believe that he is someone else, but in possession two personalities are clearly in evidence.[17] According to him this is not the case also in cases of multiple personality. It seems that when one personality in such instances is replaced by another, the consciousness of the first personality is completely blocked out.

Change in Voice

In very many cases of demon possession there is a remarkable change in the voice quality of the possessed person. This is a phenomenon that is repeatedly mentioned, perhaps because it is so obvious. Robert Peterson, who was a missionary in Borneo, says that at the new year's ceremony Chinese priests actually pray for demons to enter their bodies, and when the priest enters into the possessed state his voice no longer comes from his throat but from his stomach.[18] This may also be related to the flatulence which is mentioned by many writers in connection with demonic seizures. Peterson also speaks of a possessed woman whose voice in the possessed state came from deep in her stomach,[19] and he lists as a symptom of possession "a voice not apparently emanating from the vocal chords."[20] He says that even though he had often counselled mentally ill people, he had never heard this kind of speaking from any of them.[21]

Kurt Koch tells of a young boy who displayed the symptoms of epilepsy but who spoke in a deep voice and said, "We are three."[22] He also quotes Oesterreich as saying that a voice may suddenly change from soprano to bass[23] in a way that is beyond all explanation of medical science.[24] In 1976 a university graduate in Germany, Anneliese Michel, a pious Roman Catholic girl, apparently became possessed and an attempt at exorcism was made by two priests, who tried for ten months to drive out the devil. Forty-three tapes were made of the exorcism sessions. One of the tapes has been widely played on European television. I myself heard part of the tape in Sweden in the spring of 1977. *Time* reported that it showed Anneliese "growling obscenities, screaming guttural curses and raving wildly."[25]

The German psychiatrist, Dr. Alfred Lechler, lists a "double voice" as one of the symptoms of possession.[26]

It is, however, not only the pitch of the voice that is changed. Some observers speak of the unearthly quality of the voice that issues from the patient. Martin speaks of a "horrible voice,"[27] and several times he speaks of a voice or voices that make themselves heard in the exorcism room which seem to issue from nowhere in particular. In one place he described the voice as "mourning for an ineluctable sorrow."[28] Robert Peterson, who served as a missionary in Borneo and claims to have had experience with a number of cases of possession, says that the voice of the demon at times seems to issue not from the vocal cords but from the stomach of the possessed person.[29]

Speaking in Tongues

Coupled with this change in voice is a phenomenon that might be classified as speaking in tongues. The Roman Catholic Ritual of Exorcism lists as one of the peculiar symptoms of devil possession "when the subject speaks unknown languages with many words or understands unknown languages."[30]

That this actually happens seems to be borne out by the tape recordings made at Roman Catholic exorcisms, and it is a phenomenon often mentioned in the discussion of possession. We have noted that Marianne K., whose case is described by Malachi Martin, spoke in Hebrew, (she also spoke in Latin) and Robert Peterson speaks of a possessed woman in Borneo who was able to speak in Malay, even though she had never learned that language and was unable to speak it when she was normal.[31] Kurt Koch sees such speaking in tongues as evidence that there is a sharp distinction between insanity and possession. He writes,

> A mental patient will never be able to speak in a voice
> or a language he has previously not learned. Yet this is
> exactly what has happened and still does happen in
> many cases of possession.[32]

Something very similar is reported by Nevius who says that a Chinese Christian who had some experience with possessed people told him that people who cannot sing and those who are unable to compose poetry are able to do so with ease when in a state of possession.[33] We may be reminded here once more of what was said about Mohammed in the previous chapter.

This is something that we might keep in mind also in assessing charismatic speaking in tongues. Evidently speaking in tongues is not in itself good evidence for the presence of the Holy Spirit.

Physical Violence

Another symptom that is met frequently is physical violence. The acts of violence may be performed by the possessed person, or they may be acts of violence suffered by the possessed. The phenomenon is seen in the Scriptural accounts of possession. The Gadarene demoniac was able to break the fetters and chains with which he was bound (Mark 5:34). The account of the "epileptic" boy gives evidence of similar symptoms (Mark 9:18), and the apparently uncontrollable rages of King Saul in the Old Testament also come to mind. It will be remembered that the possessed priest whose case is described in *Hostage to the Devil* was thrown backward from the altar. Many concrete examples of such violence are found in that book. For example, in the case of Marianne K., the neighbors heard sounds of violence from her apartment for four or five hours until they finally overcame their reluctance to become involved and called the police. When the police broke down the door, they were met by a stomach curdling stench and a freezing temperature even though it was the middle of summer. The room was in complete chaos and the girl was lying on her bed with her eyes open in a coma, with blood dripping out of her mouth. When the ambulance arrived she suddenly recovered and in a normal

91

voice assured everyone that she was all right, explaining to the police that she had fallen while fixing the curtains.[34]

This manifestation of physical violence is mentioned by practically all the writers who deal with the subject of possession.

Superhuman Strength

Closely related to the physical violence that is characteristic of many cases of possession is the superhuman strength that is displayed by those possessed. The Gadarene demoniac seems to be a typical example of the sort of thing that is still met with today. A Roman Catholic exorcist is always accompanied by several strong men whose duty it is to hold the patient in order to keep him from doing violence to himself or to the exorcist. But often even strong men find it very difficult to control even a frail girl or a child. Such supernatural strength is listed in the Roman Ritual of Exorcism as one of the major indications of possession, and it is repeatedly mentioned in the literature. Kurt Koch, for example, says that it often takes three or four strong men to hold down a woman or even a child,[35] and he tells of one case in which three adults were hardly able to hold down a ten year old boy.[36]

A rather strange occurrence which does not indicate supernatural strength in the possessed but would seem to indicate a completely independent force involved is described in connection with one of the exorcisms treated in *Hostage to the Devil*. Four strong men were simply unable to lift the body of the patient from the floor to which he had fallen until the exorcist commanded the demon to cease pinning him to the ground.[37]

Obscene Language and Moral Depravity

Another symptom of possession mentioned often and demonstrated in *Hostage to the Devil* is the obscene language employed by the subject. Many years ago I once asked a fellow pastor in the Missouri Synod who served as chaplain in a mental hospital whether he thought that there might be cases of demonic possession today. He told of a girl who appeared at times to be perfectly normal but whose eyes would suddenly without warning be filled with a look of indescribable hatred and from her lips would come a torrent of obscenity. He said that she used all the dirty words he knew and many which he had never heard before; but, he said, "I could tell that they were filthy even though I did not know what

92

they meant." He also said that he knew that she could not have learned all those words in her environment. Perhaps this is another case of knowledge of a foreign language. I know also that I do not recognize many of the evidently obscene words in Martin's book. The depravity described there can only be characterized as pure, diabolic evil.

Joined with this obscene language one often finds that the life of the possessed becomes one of indescribable moral depravity.

Open Hatred of Christ and Christian Symbols

Together with this immorality goes an open hatred against Christ and all sacred things. Luther says in the Large Catechism that the devil can be driven away by making the sign of the cross. The study of demon possession would seem to underscore Luther's words. We have noted the reaction of Marianne K. when her brother hid a crucifix under her mattress. Both Protestant and Catholic writers note this aversion to all sacred things. Blasphemy against Christ and the Holy Trinity seems characteristic of demon possession. Nevius, for example, says,

> Prayer or even the reading of the Bible or some Christian book, throws the patient into a paroxysm of opposition and rage; and persistence in these exercises is almost invariably followed by the return of the subject to the normal state.[38]

In heathen countries, on the other hand, the demons often appear to be very religious and urge the people to worship their idols. The devil, as might be expected, does not oppose religion in general, but his opposition is directed against that religion which threatens his control over the hearts and minds of men.

Knowledge of Secrets

A final mark of demonization is the knowledge of secret things. Possessed people often know when the pastor is coming or if he has entered the house even if they are in a different room. Such knowledge often leads to paroxysms of violence.

During exorcism the spirits often taunt the exorcist by reminding him of secret sins which he had committed many years before, and openly proclaim those sins to the assistants of the exorcist.

Immediate Cure

One of the characteristics of possession that would be in harmony with the conclusion that a case has been correctly diagnosed as actual invasion of the personality of a human being by another personal being is found in the repeated observation that after a successful exorcism there is an immediate cure. All the abnormal and supernatural manifestations disappear, many times after an open spoken announcement on the part of the demon or demons that they are leaving. While such a radical change in behavior might be reconciled with the concept of autosuggestion or hypnosis, yet when it is coupled with the symptoms on the basis of which the diagnosis of demonization is made, it surely points also to the correctness of the conclusion that devil possession is one of the facts of life.

POLTERGEIST PHENOMENA

Closely related to the demoniac possession of persons is the possession of places. Stories of haunted houses are common in America but even more common in Europe. I suppose that all of us are inclined to write off such stories as the pure products of an overactive imagination. While we surely ought to be on our guard against naive credulity, yet the conclusions of trained observers would seem to indicate that some of these accounts are based on actual occurrences that defy a natural explanation. Parapsychologists usually speak of such "hauntings" as "poltergeist phenomena." A researcher in this field, who does not believe in the existence of spirits, nevertheless says,

> The reality of this ghostly force is still controversial;
> but to many of those engaged in parapsychological
> studies, it is thoroughly documented, and its existence
> is beyond dispute.[39]

The German word "polter" means to "cause noise by knocking things about." A poltergeist, therefore, is a ghost that knocks objects around in a noisy way. The phenomenon is aptly named.

According to reports that occasionally appear in the newspapers and that have often been investigated, strange and unexplained events take place as a result of haunting by a poltergeist. Unusual noises are heard for which there is no explanation. They are described as moanings, groanings, scratching, pounding, rapping, and even actual speech. Dishes rattle or even fly around the room.

Rocks whose source is obscure fall or are thrown. Sometimes they fall slowly in apparent violation of the law of gravity, or they fly in a curved pattern that cannot be accounted for by any of the laws of motion. When the rocks are picked up, they are found to be either unnaturally hot or cold. Heavy furniture is moved without anyone being near it. Objects mysteriously appear or disappear. The temperature of a room may be mysteriously raised or lowered. Fires, for which there is no apparent cause, may be kindled, and sometimes floods of water appear from nowhere. Sometimes apparitions are seen which are identified as previous tenants in the house or castle, very often people who have been murdered or committed suicide. Strong odors often manifest themselves.

Many of these phenomena are associated with spiritism and devil possession. Martin, for example, says that in the presence of a possessed person

> objects fly about the room; wallpaper peels off the walls; furniture cracks; crockery breaks, there are strange rumblings, hisses, and other noises with no apparent source. Often the temperature in the room where the possessed happens to be will drop dramatically. Even more often an acrid and distinctive stench accompanies the person.[40]

Even people who accept the supernatural find it difficult to believe that such things really happen and that they are caused by spirits, or, if they do suspect that they might be true, they may find it difficult in this materialistic age to admit to such secret doubts about the closed character of this universe of ours.

But the explanations for the cases that cannot be accounted for naturally, given by those who deny the spiritual origin of the phenomena, are even harder to believe. Because the unnatural occurrences often are associated with specific individuals, especially children, and because the strange happenings often cease when the person with whom they are associated is removed from the house, or are even transferred to his new residence, it is concluded that there is a mysterious force in the individual involved. Some scientists speak of "disassociation" as an explanation. According to this view, frustrations or resentments in the child become motivating forces that operate outside the child in a way that would seem to indicate that they have a separate existence. Anyone who can believe that "scientific" explanation should find it easy to believe in spirits.

To deal with the problem, sometimes spiritistic mediums are engaged to contact the poltergeist and persuade it to leave. Sometimes they appear to be successful. In heathen countries offerings and sacrifices made to the spirits sometimes seem to remove the annoyance. In Christian countries the houses are exorcised and the spirits are commanded to leave in Jesus' name. The Catholic Church has a special ritual for the exorcism of places. This, too, is said to bring an end to the "haunting" in many cases.

THE CAUSES OF DEVIL POSSESSION

Not much is said in the literature about the causes of devil possession. In a general way, of course, we must say that when Adam and Eve listened to the suggestions of Satan in the garden they opened the door to the influence of the devil in the lives of their descendants.

The dogmaticians also see a close connection between the ability of the devil to enlist men in the service of sin and what we today call devil possession. In fact, they view all unbelievers as being, in a sense, devil possessed. They have biblical justification for this view. For that reason also the old Lutheran liturgy of baptism contained an exorcism, which in most Lutheran liturgies survives only in the question, "Do you renounce the devil with all his works and all his ways?" The Lutheran Confessional Church in Sweden, because of the widespread denial of the existence of the devil and original sin, has reinstituted the exorcism in the baptismal liturgy as a protest against that unbelief.

While it is difficult to pinpoint specific causes for demonization in its extraordinary form, it would seem that the consent of the possessed is somehow necessary. Some people, who become possessed, consciously permit and even invite the devil to make use of their physical and mental faculties. It is a rather common practice for witch doctors and heathen priests to invite demons to take over control of their minds and bodies.

Those who have made a study of demoniac possession often speak of the use of drugs as a factor in the onset of the affliction. Experimentation with divination and spiritism are also often in the background. Even exorcism of others may contribute to the possession of the exorcist. The possessed parapsychologist in *Hos-*

tage to the Devil seems to have started down the road to possession by the practice of something that sounds very much like Transcendental Meditation. The literature of the occult often speaks of the need for passivity on the part of those who want to be successful in the practice of the various occult arts, whether they be divination, magic, or spiritism. The passive state promoted by Transcendental Meditation, as well as other forms of yoga, would seem to open the door for demonic influences to invade the mind. In fact, the more advanced yoga states manifest many of the same symptoms as demonic possession.

Something might also be said about the role of music in inducing possession. Students of voodoo have noted the possession by spirits is brought about in part at least by certain musical rhythms, and anyone who has witnessed the effect of some types of modern music on an impressionable audience may, after having studied various facets of the occult, be excused for seeing in those effects some type of diabolic influence. It might be of some value to the church if someone who is competent in the area of music would make a special study of the relation between music and demonic possession. It certainly seems to be true that certain types of music often play a great role in producing what are described widely today as charismatic experiences.

It seems also that when the devil seeks to gain possession he makes all kinds of promises or threats to the intended victim. The persons approached may not be fully aware of the nature of the temptation, and yet, after exorcism, they often admit that they knew that it was something evil. That at least tacit acceptance of the condition of possession is necessary is asserted by Martin, who writes, "At every new step, and during every moment of possession, the consent of the victim is necessary, or possession cannot be successful."[41] This, at least in the case of Christians, agrees with the Scriptural injunction, "Resist the devil, and he will flee from you" (James 4:7).

There is one feature in the onset of possession that I wish I had paid more attention to from the beginning. I do not know whether it is significant, but in a number of cases people who later appear to have been possessed had spirit playmates when they were children. Edgar Cayce's secretary reports that in his childhood he played with fairies and elves.[42] This point is also made in the novel *The Exorcist.*

EXORCISM

In all cultures attempts are made to cure devil possession by means of exorcism. In heathen countries this is done by magic spells and charms or by inflicting pain on the possessed person.[43] Something similar to this we meet in the apocryphal book of Tobit, where the smell of the burning liver and heart of a fish drives the demon away (Tob. 6:16). Josephus tells of exorcisms which he had witnessed in which incantations were used that had supposedly been composed by Solomon (Antiq. VIII, 2).

In the Bible, exorcism is a rather simple process. The Savior and the apostles spoke a short word of command to the demons and a cure immediately followed. It would surely be indicated by all that we know of the matter from Scripture that if exorcism is to be practiced at all, it ought to be still such a simple affair. The German expert on possession T. K. Oesterreich said that in certain areas of the foreign mission field, "Christians have had the courage when faced with possessed persons, calmly to command in the name of Christ the evil spirit to depart, for it is a matter of course to them that the demon will then leave the unfortunate person."[44] Nevius also records a number of instances in China in which possession was cured by prayer in the name of Jesus.

Most of the exorcisms which have come to the attention of the general public in our time have been performed by Roman Catholic priests. The case of exorcism described in the novel *The Exorcist* is based on an actual case in which a Roman priest exorcised a Lutheran boy. This is also the case in every one of the exorcisms described by Martin in *Hostage to the Devil.*

In times gone by, every Roman diocese had an official exorcist and this is still true today in most major dioceses, according to Martin. Before any exorcism may be legitimately performed, however, the exorcist must have the consent of the bishop. Before such permission is given the subject must receive a thorough medical and psychiatric examination to establish the fact that neither physical nor mental illness is involved.

When permission is given and a place for the exorcism has been chosen, the room is prepared for the actual rite. It is recommended that all movable objects be removed from the room and that the windows be covered or boarded up. Only a bed or couch and a small table on which are placed a crucifix, candles, holy water, a prayer book, and a relic or picture of a saint are left. In many modern exorcisms a tape recorder is used to preserve a complete record of the session.

The exorcist is usually accompanied by an assisting priest and four laymen whose duty is to hold down the victim if he should become violent. Martin says that the assistants must be people who are able to endure foul and obscene language, blood, excrement, and urine, and that they must be prepared to have their darkest secrets screeched in public. These, he says, are routine happenings in exorcisms.[45] They must also be persons of great stamina; for a Roman Catholic exorcism is a long-drawn-out process, lasting for many hours, sometimes for several days. Often, too, the exorcism sessions are repeated over a period of weeks or months. One case, already alluded to earlier and recently reported in *Time Magazine*,[46] was carried on for ten months. During the course of the exorcism forty-three tapes were made of the sessions.

The Roman Church has an official ritual of exorcism, which need, however, not be followed strictly, since according to Roman doctrine, the rite is not a sacrament and therefore its efficacy does not depend on the exact repetition of the forms but depends rather on the faith of the exorcist. The exorcist says a mass before the exorcism begins. The "Litany of the Saints" is recited by the exorcist and his assistants, after which the spirit is summoned and commanded in the name of God to make himself known. Gospel selections are read and the exorcist lays his hands on the patient with a prayer for his recovery. The evil spirit is then directly addressed and special note is taken of words or phrases which cause the most violent reaction so that they may be repeated often to cause the demon as much distress as possible. The Athanasian creed is recited and psalms are read.

When the pretense of the spirit has been broken down and he admits his presence, he is asked for his name and then finally he is commanded to leave and never return.

It will be evident immediately that a Roman Catholic exorcism bears little resemblance to the simple biblical accounts of the casting out of devils. While the biblical reports are a clear demonstration of the power of the name of Jesus, the Roman rite lays far greater stress on the power of the exorcist. It is true that the name of Jesus is considered to have great power, but it is difficult to escape the impression that it appears to be used almost like a magical incantation, especially in view of the Roman doctrine that the efficacy of the rite depends upon the authorization of the church authorities and the faith of the exorcist.[47] One thing that is made clear by every one of Martin's cases is this that in the final analysis the ultimate success of the exorcism depends on the staying power of the exorcist. Martin says that there are six stages that are passed through in exorcism. The one immediately preceding the expulsion is called the "clash," which he says is a struggle of will between the priest and the demon to force the demon to give its name.[48] The relation between this approach to the Roman doctrine of salvation will be obvious.

One other great difference between biblical and Roman Catholic exorcism is indicated also by the title of Martin's book. The title *Hostage to the Devil* has reference to the Roman view that the priestly exorcist offers himself literally as a hostage to the devil in order to fight in behalf of the exorcee the battle he cannot fight for himself. The Roman doctrine of the priestly office is clearly mirrored in that conception.

Coupled with that emphasis on the priest as a very special mediator between men and the world of the unseen, is the theme that recurs often in Roman exorcisms, namely, that in performing exorcisms a priest suffers physical or psychical damage. In the book, *The Exorcist,* the priest performing the exorcism dies. In one of Martin's cases, the priest himself becomes at least partially possessed. Such conceptions surely do not accord with the biblical doctrine that Christ has destroyed the power of the devil over his people.

That may not mean that a Christian cannot be possessed. That question, which we will discuss in more detail later in this book, we may never be able to decide absolutely this side of eternity. But we can rest assured that a Christian who fights this battle in the faith that Christ has set us free from the old evil foe will be victorious finally over every diabolic onslaught.

He can harm us none.
He's judged; the deed is done.
One little word can fell him.

SOURCES
Chapter IV

1. Rudolf Bultmann, "A Reply to the Theses of J. Schniewind," in Hans Werner Bartsch, *Kerygma and Myth,* New York, Harper Torchbooks, 1961, p. 120.
2. David Farren, op. cit. p. 88.
3. Malachi Martin, *Hostage to the Devil,* New York, Reader's Digest Press, 1976, p. 298.
4. Martin, op. cit. 11.
5. Michelet, op. cit., p. 171.
6. Baroja, op. cit., pp. 138.
7. Kurt Koch, *Christian Counselling and Occultism,* p. 300.
8. Martin, op. cit., p. 11.
9. John B. Nevius, *Demon Possession,* Grand Rapids, Kregel, 1968, p. 9.
10. Martin, op. cit., p. 24.
11. Ibid., p. 58.
12. Ibid., p. 59.
13. Ibid., p. 62.
14. Ibid., p. 246.
15. Ibid., p. 35.
16. Quoted in Kurt Koch, *Christian Counselling and Occultism,* p. 246.
17. Unger, *Demon Possession,* p. 103f.
18. R. Peterson, *Are Demons for Real?* Chicago, Moody Press, 1973, p. 16.
19. Ibid., p. 52f.
20. Ibid., p. 116.
21. Ibid., p. 117f.
22. Kurt Koch, *Occult Bondage,* pp. 8f.
23. Ibid., pp. 216f.
24. *Christian Counselling and Occultism,* p. 251.
25. *Time,* 108,10 (Sept. 6, 1976), p. 68.
26. *Christian Counselling and Occultism,* p. 256.
27. Op. cit., p. 241.
28. Ibid., p. 244.
29. Robert Peterson, *Are Demons for Real,* Chicago: Moody Press, 1972, pp. 116ff.
30. Martin, op. cit., p. 460.
31. Op. cit., p. 117.
32. *Occult Bondage* and *Deliverance,* p. 58f.
33. Nevius, op. cit., p. 58.
34. Martin, op. cit., pp. 55f.
35. *Christian Counselling,* p. 217.
36. Ibid., p. 251.
37. Op. cit., p. 305.
38. Nevius, op. cit., p. 194.

39. Raymond Bayless, *The Enigma of the Poltergeist*, West Nyack, New York, 1967, p. VI.
40. Martin, op. cit., p. 10.
41. Ibid., p. 436.
42. Carter, op. cit., p. 73.
43. Nevius, op. cit., p. 54.
44. Kurt Koch, *Christian Counselling* p. 250.
45. Op. cit., pp. 12,16.
46. *Time*, Sept. 6, 1976 (108,10) p. 68.
47. Martin, op. cit., p. 459.
48. Ibid., p. 21.

5

Satanism

"All these things will I give thee, if thou wilt fall down and worship me."
                                                                    Matt. 4:9.

"The things which the Gentiles sacrifice, they sacrifice to devils."
                                                                    1 Cor. 10:20

"They overcame him (the devil) by the blood of the Lamb, and by the word of their testimony."
                                                                    Rev. 12:11.

The final stage in involvement with the occult is Satanism, the actual overt worship of the devil. What may have begun as curiosity about the reliability of astrological predictions may easily end in actually falling down before Satan to worship him.

THE EVIL ANGELS IN SCRIPTURE

That there are evil angels who are real, personal beings is the clear teaching of the Bible.

Many false views concerning the origin of evil angels have been proposed. Some hold that evil angels have existed from eternity. Others say that the evil angels are the souls of evil men who lived in worlds created and destroyed before our world was made.

The Bible, however, clearly teaches that all angels were created by God. Paul writes, "By him were all things created, that are in heaven, and that are in earth, visible and invisible" (Col 1:16). While, therefore, also the devils are creatures of God, they were not created evil. At the end of the sixth day everything that God had made at the beginning was still "very good" (Gn 1:31).

But sometime after the close of the sixth day of creation some of the good angels sinned (2 Peter 2:4). Through their fall into sin they lost their place in heaven. Jude says that they kept not their "first estate." The word translated "first estate" literally means either "beginning" or "rule." The word may therefore imply that these were highly placed angels who occupied positions of authority in the armies of heaven, but of this we can not be certain. Jesus says that the devil did not remain "in the truth." For that reason also the devil is called the "father of lies." Untruth, false doctrine, is one of the chief tools by which the devil does his work.

That does not mean that the devil never tells the truth. When he tempted Eve in the Garden of Eden, most of his statements to Eve were true. But within the layers of truth he sandwiched the lie that Adam and Eve would not die if they disobeyed God and by that lie he persuaded Eve to believe that her full happiness lay not in what God in His grace and mercy had provided for them but in what she could gain for herself by what she did. The whole concept of salvation by works rather than by grace alone was thus introduced into the world.

SATAN

The leader of the evil angels is called Satan. This is really a Hebrew word which means "adversary" or "enemy," "the one who opposes." He is above all the enemy of God but also the adversary of God's people (1 Peter 5:8). His intent is to bring all of God's works to ruin, especially to bring eternal destruction upon men by leading them into sin and unbelief.

The word "devil" is derived from the Greek word "diabolos," which means "slanderer." Even though in modern English the word "devil" has become a common noun, it is originally a proper name. The Greek word is never used in the plural form in the New Testament. Thus the New Testament, strictly speaking, mentions only one Devil. Wherever our English translation has the plural form "devils" the original Greek has the word "daimonia" or "demons."

The devil is also called, in the book of Revelation, Apollyon or Abaddon (Rev. 9:11). The first is a Greek word and the second Hebrew, both meaning "Destroyer." In the same passage he is called "the angel of the bottomless pit." In a later chapter of the same book he is called "the great dragon" and "the old serpent" (Rev. 2:9). This last name is certainly derived from the story of the fall in which the devil spoke to Eve in the form of a serpent.

Whether the name Lucifer, which is often used today as a name for the devil, is a name given to Satan in the Bible is questionable.

The name is found in the book of Isaiah (14:12), and is often understood as a reference to the devil, but the context seems to indicate that the prophet is here speaking not to the devil but to the city of Babylon. Some commentators believe that in the directions concerning the great day of atonement (Lev. 16:8) the Hebrew word Azazel, which in the King James version is translated "scapegoat," is a name for the devil, but this is, to say the least, by no means certain.

A common New Testament name for the devil is Beelzebub. This was originally the name of a heathen god "Baal-zebub" (2 Kings 1:2). The original form of the name is not completely certain. It was either "Baal-zebul," meaning "Lord of the dwelling," or "Baal-zebub," which means "Lord of flies." The fact that the name of a heathen god became the name of the devil illustrates Paul's statement that the sacrifices of the heathen are offered to devils (1 Cor. 10:20).

The name Belial, used in the New Testament and in later Christian terminology as a name for the devil, originally was a Hebrew word meaning "worthlessness." It is not always certain whether the phrase "sons of Belial" in the Old Testament means "sons of the devil" or simply "worthless or wicked people."

Satan is also called "the tempter" (Matt. 4:3), "the wicked one" (Matt. 13:9), "the prince of this world" (John 12:31) or "the god of this world" (2 Cor. 4:4) or "the prince of the power of the air" (Eph. 2:2). The reasons for the first two names are obvious, while the last three all speak of the power that the devil has gained over men and this present world through the fall into sin.

CHRIST AND SATAN

Jesus was manifested to destroy the works of the devil (1 John 3:8). By His holy life and innocent death He undid the damage done by the devil in the Garden of Eden. By atoning for our sins He made it impossible for the devil to accuse us before the judgment throne of God (Rev. 12:7-11). Thus He crushed the head of the old serpent (Gen. 3:16) and set men free from the power of the devil.

Yet the Bible also teaches that until the day of judgment, when the devil will be permanently cast out so that he will no longer be able to harm God's people in any way (Rev. 20:10), the devil roams this earth as a roaring lion, seeking to destroy also the children of God (1 Peter 5:8). However, the Scriptures also assure us that those who put their trust in Christ will triumph over Satan. Our sins, which alone give the devil power over men, have been forgiven and washed away by the blood of Christ.

THE PREVALENCE OF SATANISM IN THE MODERN WORLD

It may seem strange that men should have any desire to worship the devil. That the devil desires to receive worship from men is made clear by his temptation of Jesus (Matt. 4:8,9; Luke 4:5-7).

Devil worship, in spite of the publicity which it is receiving at the present time, is not something new under the sun. Through the ages devil cults, such as the Himiko cult in Japan, have maintained themselves more or less openly in heathen countries. Baroja says that the devil has been worshiped and is still worshiped today in the Basque country of Spain.[1]

But in our time Satanism has become more bold and visible. A name that keeps recurring in the literature on Satanism is that of Aleister Crowley, a depraved and debauched Englishman who found delight in shocking his fellowmen, who took pride in his depravity, who called himself the wickedest man in the world and whose own mother called the great beast whose coming was foretold in the book of Revelation.[2] His motto by which he lived was, "Do what thou wilt shall be the whole of the law." The account of his depravity is a boring recital of drug abuse, pornography, homosexuality, fornication, witchcraft, and ends with a miserable death in 1947. He founded a religion, which he called Crowleyanity, which is today being revived, especially on college campuses. According to Wm. Peterson, Crowley has "done more to popularize Satanism in this century than any other man."[3]

Since most Satanism, however, is still carried on more or less in secret, it is impossible to gain a comprehensive picture of the prevalence or the nature of this type of worship. From time to time evidence of Satanistic practices are uncovered by the police and reported in the newspapers. Perhaps the most celebrated case is the Manson murder of Sharon Tate. There seem to be indications that the people present in the house with Sharon Tate and murdered with her may have been engaged also in Satanistic practices. Sharon Tate's husband was the man who directed the film, *Rosemary's Baby*. It is known that Manson claimed that he was an incarnation of the devil and openly asserted that all the women associated with him were witches.

Many other murders and the apparently ritual killing of countless animals are viewed by the police as evidence of devil worship. There seems, for example, to be no other explanation for the large number of dog bodies drained of all blood that have been found in northern California.[4] One visible manifestation of the prevalence of Satanistic practices is to be found in the fact that almost all of our larger cities have a Satanistic bookstore. It is almost impossible also to distinguish clearly between Satanism and witchcraft at times.

TYPES OF SATANISM

The sociologist Marcello Truzzi speaks of two types of Satanism found in America today, which he calls "solitary" and "group" Satanism. Concerning the first type he says that we know very little because it is almost always secret. Group Satanism he again divides into Gnostic groups, which consider the devil as an angel to be worshiped, sex clubs, which practice the black mass, narcotic groups such as the Manson family, and the Church of Satan. He says also that most of the literature on Satanism is unreliable, but I have the impression that at least one reason for his opinion lies in the fact that he would consider any report of the supernatural to be unreliable.

THE CHURCH OF SATAN

The Church of Satan is by far the most visible of all the Satanistic groups. It was founded in 1966 by Anton Szandor La Vey. The church is incorporated under the laws of California and has received tax exempt status from the Internal Revenue Service. By 1969 La Vey was claiming 7,000 contributing members. Wm. Petersen's book, *Those Curious New Cults,* which was copyrighted in 1972, reported that the church had 10,000 adherents. The individual congregations are called "grottos," and in 1969 Tiryakian reported that La Vey expected to have grottos in every state by 1971.

La Vey calls himself the high priest of Satanism and has received a great deal of free publicity both from the press and the television networks. He played the part of the devil in the film *Rosemary's Baby.* He has written a number of books, the best-known of which is *The Satanic Bible,* which reportedly outsells the Holy Bible in some bookstores. Hundreds of thousands of copies have been sold, and in 1976 the tenth printing was being offered for sale by booksellers.

Edward J. Moody investigated the Church of Satan by participating in its worship services for two years. He found that many of the members exhibited pathological behavior, homosexualism, sadism, masochism, and transvestism. He says that all novices who applied for membership demonstrated a high level of anxiety in their lives and that 85 per cent came from broken homes. Almost all of them had experienced failure in love, business, or social relationships and had tried other forms of the occult such as astrology, the Tarot, or spiritualism, before turning to Satanism.[5] Those scientific findings are surely of some significance also for the church.

Strangely enough, La Vey denies the objective existence of Satan, and holds that the Christian churches have been able to maintain their existence only by pretending that Satan exists. Yet he holds that men need some kind of ritual to satisfy a natural urge to worship. At the same time he maintains that the only honest form of worship is that which admits that the object of worship is a myth.

One would suppose that such a program would be self-defeating, but C. S. Lewis said something to the effect that one of the most effective lies of the devil is to convince men that he does not exist. We might say of La Vey's brand of Satanism what E. A. Hooten said of evolution, namely, that it frees men from religious inhibitions and fears which alone make them socially tolerable. And therein lies much of its appeal for sinful men. La Vey openly champions the crassest kind of self-indulgence by assuring men that God, who is only a mythological being, does not care what they do, and the devil as a personal being does not exist. At the same time he holds that both God and Satan exist in the sense that they are names that we use to denote naturalistic forces in the universe.

La Vey summarizes the principle teachings of his church in the so-called "Nine Satanic Statements," namely

1. Satan represents indulgence, instead of abstinence!
2. Satan represents vital existence, instead of spiritual

pipe dreams!

3. Satan represents undefiled wisdom, instead of hypo-
critical self-deceit!

4. Satan represents kindness to those who deserve it,
instead of love wasted on ingrates!

5. Satan represents vengeance, instead of turning the
other cheek!

6. Satan represents responsibility to the responsible,
instead of concern for psychic vampires!

7. Satan represents man as just another animal, sometimes better, more often worse than those who walk
on all-fours, who, because of his "divine spiritual and
intellectual development," has become the most vi-
cious animal of all!

8. Satan represents all the so-called sins, as they all
lead to physical, mental, or emotional gratification!

9. Satan has been the best friend the church has ever
had, as he has kept it in business all these years!

La Vey delights in blaspheming the God of the Bible and ridi-
culing the teachings of Christianity. I debated with myself whether one ought even to repeat the diabolical blasphemies that are
found in the *Satanic Bible*, but perhaps a few of his blasphemies
will help men see the depth of moral depravity that he represents
and also the moral decay of a society that accords respectability to
such men. He speaks of the "watery blood of your impotent mad
redeemer," "the worm-eaten skull of Jehovah," and says that the
crucifix symbolizes "pallid incompetence hanging on a tree." One
is reminded of the blasphemies of demoniacs, and it may be that
La Vey is a person who might be called "totally possessed," in
whom none of the symptoms of violence usually associated with
possession are found because there is no part of his personality
still struggling against the devil's will.

His moral teachings are, for the most part, an unimaginative
but blasphemous reversal of Christian principles. He asks, "Why
should I not hate mine enemies?" and "Is it natural for enemies to
do good unto each other?" "Love your enemies and do good to
them that hate and use you — is this not the despicable philosophy
of the spaniel that rolls upon its back when kicked?" He answers

109

his own questions by saying, "Hate your enemies with a whole heart, and if a man smite you on one cheek, SMASH him on the other! . . . He who turns the other cheek is a cowardly dog!" The *Satanic Bible* has its own set of beatitudes, one of which reads, "Blessed are those who believe in what is best for them, for never shall their minds be terrorized — Cursed are the 'lambs of God,' for they shall be bled whiter than snow."

La Vey advocates complete devotion to the gratification of the flesh. The virtues of Satanism, according to him, are the seven deadly sins of the church. Envy and greed, for example, are virtues because they are the motivating forces of ambition, without which very little could be accomplished. Lust is necessary to insure the propagation of the human race. With such arguments, which are in reality only a specific application of the philosophy of pragmatism, he seeks to persuade men that what the church has called sin is really good. Satanism, he says, "represents a form of controlled selfishness. This does not mean that you never do anything for anyone else. If you do something to make someone for whom you care happy, his happiness will give you a sense of gratification." Thus even altruism, for La Vey, is only another form of selfishness. He is, of course, correct about much of the altruism displayed in the world.

On the other hand, he ridicules magic if it is understood as a spiritual power. He opposes the use of drugs because they really interfere with self-gratification in the long run. He defends the movement against the charge that it encourages sex orgies and extra-marital affairs, by saying that such activities are not recommended to those to whom they do not come naturally. He says that a Satanist would never perform a human sacrifice unless such a sacrifice would release the magician's wrath and free the world of an obnoxious person who deserves to die. La Vey, for example, claims responsibility for the death of lawyer Sam Brody, on whom he pronounced a curse because of his influence over Jayne Mansfield, who was a member of La Vey's Church of Satan. He evidently did not intend to kill Jayne Mansfield, who was decapitated in the accident that killed Brody.

Thus while La Vey ridicules magic if it is understood to be a spiritual force, he nevertheless believes in magic as the employment of natural forces to obtain what is unavailable to you by normally accepted methods. Half of the Satanic Bible is devoted to in-

110

struction in the performance of magic and the incantations and spells that are used. La Vey believes that when a group of people together will a certain thing to happen, then, if the magic is properly worked, the desired result will come to pass. The invocation to Satan which is spoken at the beginning of the magic ritual is, according to him, only intended to elevate the emotional pitch of those participating in the ritual, since magic is essentially the release of emotions that act as independent forces against or in behalf of the objects toward which they are directed.

THE BLACK MASS

Associated with Satanism through the ages is the so-called "black mass." Because the ritual of the black mass was in times past performed in secret, the origin of the custom is not clearly known, but it can be traced back to the middle of the 17th century in France. In the 18th century it was practiced in England, and has become part and parcel of modern Satanism in America.

The ritual of the black mass is too vile to be described in detail. The altar at a black mass is the naked body of a woman. The chalice is filled with wine which is mixed with the blood of a cat or some other animal or person and sometimes also with the urine of a prostitute. The wafer is often made of bread heavily laced with drugs. The crucifix is displayed over the altar upside down. If possible, a defrocked priest officiates at the mass. The Scriptures are read backwards. In fact, everything conceivable is done to parody and ridicule the Lord's Supper.

The black mass usually ends in a sexual orgy. In fact, in many cases the mass is used to break down whatever inhibitions the participants may have to the most depraved and unnatural sexual perversions. Wm. Petersen quotes an occultist as saying that "the wife swapping clubs that are springing up in middle class suburban neighborhoods across the country are increasingly being converted into Satanic covens."[6] When we realize that some of the members of Christian congregations have become involved in that sort of activity, we must surely recognize that Satanism is not something so far removed from us to constitute no danger to God's people, who ought to be warned to resist the beginnings.

A Protestant evangelist has told of his own involvement in Satanism as a high priest of the cult.[7] For him involvement in Satanism began with the smoking of marijuana and a desire to be accepted by a group of young people he met at the university. His story would seem to indicate that we need not only warn our young people against the kind of *teaching* that they will meet in the secondary schools of our country but also against the kind of *people* with whom they might come into contact on the campus.

THE BIBLE AND DEVIL WORSHIP

Before we leave the subject of Satanism we ought to say at least a few words about the Bible and devil worship. If my memory serves me well, the only passage in Scripture that speaks of overt worship of the devil is the account of the temptation in the wilderness, where Jesus was tempted to fall down in worship before the devil.

But we ought not to forget the words of Paul, when he says, "The things which the Gentiles sacrifice, they sacrifice to devils (demons) and not to God" (1 Cor. 10:20). Paul says earlier in the same letter that an idol is nothing in this world (1 Cor. 8:4) and the Bible often speaks of idols as lying vanities. Yet there is no reason why we should say that Paul is employing figurative language when he says that the Gentiles offer sacrifices to devils, and perhaps Milton's practice of giving the devils in *Paradise Lost* the names of false gods mentioned in the Old Testament is closer to the truth than we sometimes realize. In the various forms of the occult we may actually be seeing demons at work seeking worship for themselves. In heathen countries the demons of possessed persons often actually make a demand for worship and sacrifice price for the cessation of violence and suffering.

In that same vein, when Paul speaks of "seducing spirits" and "doctrines of devils" (1 Tim. 4:1) may we not assume that the false doctrines that plague the church are actually "inspired" by evil spirits intent upon leading God's people away from the truth? As we have seen earlier, there is some evidence that Mohammedanism is such a demonic religion. We might also ask whether it is necessary for us to assume that the angel Moroni in Mormonism is a pure product of Joseph Smith's imagination. In that connection some light may be cast on what Paul says here by a story told by Andrija Puharich in his book on Uri Geller. Puharich says that in 1951 he had a meeting with a Dr. Vinod from India. Vinod went into a trance in which he spoke in a deep sonorous voice in perfect English, although normally he spoke faulty English with an ac-

112

cent in a high-pitched soft voice. Among other things, Puharich quotes Vinod as saying.

> Remember, all this is a real guidance from God. God is nobody else than we together, the Nine Principles of God. There is no God other than what we are together. And just for once in your lifetime believe this to be the truth. If God ever spoke, if God ever made an instrument of a human being — it is now that he has made it; and look upon this as the most precious moment in your lives. These are God's words.[8]

Puharich was then told by the voice that came out of Vinod's mouth that if mankind was to be saved it would take the cooperative efforts of man and the "nine principles of God" which were revealing themselves to him through Vinod. The great lie of the devil is again clearly discernable, for again man is told to find his salvation through human effort rather than through God's free and faithful grace.

While Satanism shocks us, we ought to remember that the occult in all its ramifications is not the most dangerous deception of the devil. Spiritism, divination, magic, witchcraft, possession are only spectacular examples of something far more subtle and far more dangerous that goes on every day all around us. It is still true, as St. Paul reminds us, that the god of this world has blinded the minds of those who do not believe (2 Cor. 5:4) and that those who oppose the pure doctrine have fallen into the snare of the devil who takes them captive at his will (2 Tim. 2:26). The daily sins to which the devil constantly tempts men and the false doctrines by which he leads them astray, entirely apart from all occult manifestations, these lead far greater numbers to destruction than real or imagined supernatural occurrences.

Our strongest weapon against all the wiles of the devil is the Word of God in which God has revealed to us all we need to know about the secret things of the supernatural world. Children of God who know that they have a God who loves them and who governs the world in such a way that all things, even the sorrows and the tragedies of life, work together for good for those who love God, will not need the doubtful kind of assurance about the future that can be offered by astrologers and diviners of every sort, even if they may be right in 75 per cent of their predictions. Children of God who have learned to pray in childlike faith, "Thy will be done," will not seek to frustrate that will by charms and incantations. Those who know that in His Word God has revealed all that we need for our instruction, hope, and comfort and that He has in that same Word told us all that we need to know of that "undiscovered country from whose bourn no traveller returns," will not seek unto "wizards that peep and that mutter" in spiritistic trance. Those who have learned to believe that the promises of forgiveness and salvation are universal and sure will not need the assurance to be found in human experience, even in such spectacular phenomena as speaking in tongues and healing miracles, especially when they know that these supernatural signs of the Holy Spirit's presence can be mimicked and have been mimicked by the devil.

Our best defense against the modern explosion of the occult is therefore not more knowledge of the occult on our part or on the part of those whom we may have been called to teach, even though shepherds of God's people ought not to be ignorant of the devices of the devil. Neither is it enough to tell people that involvement in the occult, depending on where we draw the line in our definition, either is a clear violation of God's commands or can very easily become that. Nor is our best defense against the wiles of the devil to be found in this that we learn to "live close to Christ," as *Christianity Today* said in an editorial a few months ago,[9] for even occult involvement is seen by some as coming closer to Christ.

As in our dealing with every type of human depravity, the best weapon is the Gospel of God's redeeming love in Christ who has come to destroy all the works of the devil and whose death and resurrection has torn the veil before the holy of holies so that we now have a clear view into the heart of that hidden God who revealed Himself to Moses as the God who forgives sin and the God who punishes sin and has found a way to do both in one and the same act on Calvary's holy mountain. Those who have come to know that mystery, which was hidden and "kept secret since the world began," as Paul says (Rom. 16:25), will be able to curb that sinful curiosity that forgets that "the secret things belong unto the Lord our God; but those things which are revealed belong unto us and to our children forever" (Deut. 29:29).

114

CONCLUSION

THE CHRISTIAN PASTOR AND THE OCCULT

If a Christian pastor is truly to serve as the shepherd of the flock that God has entrusted to him in the modern world, he can scarcely ignore completely the intense interest in the occult. He certainly also ought to learn to recognize it in its various forms, so that he may be able to warn his people against occult involvement.

In dealing with the matter in general, however, we might well keep in mind the words of Moses, "The secret things belong to the Lord our God; but those things which are revealed belong unto us and to our children forever" (Deut. 29:29). The occult is really only another name for the secret things, the supernatural, of which only God has true knowledge. In speaking of these things we ought therefore once more remind ourselves that we can have true knowledge of the supernatural only from the revelation of God that we have in the verbally inspired and inerrant Word of our God. This means, of course, that we will be careful not to be guided by our own notions of what is possible or impossible, on the one hand, and on the other, that we will pay close attention to exactly what the Bible says.

CAN AN UNBELIEVER CAST OUT DEVILS?

There are many questions that are asked repeatedly to which the Bible does not give a direct answer and with which we ought to deal most carefully lest we give an answer based more on logical argument than on God's Word. In pastoral care and concern the shepherds of God's people should also always be aware of the implications of such questions and the answers which they give to them. More is often involved than just satisfying someone's curiosity. For example, I began the study of the occult with the notion that no unbeliever could ever cast out a devil, since Christ says in the Gospel that if Satan cast out Satan (Matt. 12:26),[10] his kingdom can not stand. When we then read of apparently successful exorcisms performed by heathen sorcerers or by Roman Catholic exorcists operating, in large measure, with prayers to the Virgin and to the saints, we seem to be forced to the conclusion that apparently competent witnesses have been deceived or that they are practicing deception.

But it may also be that we have not been alert enough to the ex-

115

act wording of the biblical statement concerning the casting out of devils. For members of the Wisconsin Synod, who have fought a great battle in the past decades for the verbal inspiration and inerrancy of the Bible, the exact wording of Scripture ought to be important and significant. It should be noted that the Bible never speaks of exorcism as being an exercise by which *Satan* is cast out. There is also no passage dealing with exorcism which speaks of *the devil's* being cast out. When the Bible speaks of the casting out of Satan this is always a reference to something far greater than any exorcism. Jesus cast out or cast down the devil or Satan by His death and resurrection (John 12:31), which free us finally from all the power of the devil, and the exorcism miracles in the Gospel serve their intended purpose when they point us to the victory over Satan at the cross and the open tomb.

The AV version confuses the issue by using the word "devil" where the original has the word "demon." The so-called "devils" who are cast out are always described as "spirits," "unclean spirits" or "demons." In the light of that usage it may not be pedantic to point out that Jesus did not say, "If Satan cast out demons, his kingdom can not stand." We might therefore ask whether it is inconceivable that the devil, who is portrayed in the Bible as the father of lies and as the ruler of the evil angels or demons, does sometimes order his inferiors to obey an exorcist if it suits his evil purpose to do so.

After all, the Bible does tell us that when the Antichrist is revealed his coming will be "according to the working of Satan" with all kinds of "miracles and signs and lying wonders" (2 Thess. 2:9). Are we to understand the "lying wonders" of the Roman Catholic church to be lies in the sense that they do not really take place but are pure invention? Or are they ever truly supernatural occurrences that come to pass through the power of Satan in the service of the great lie of salvation by works, which he introduced into the world when he persuaded Eve that her happiness did not consist in what God had done for her but in what she could do for herself? And if the miracles of the Roman Church are done by the power of Satan and serve the purposes of Satan, would Satan be casting out Satan in a Roman exorcism if he ordered one of his own to leave a body in which it had taken up residence?

What is said about Roman exorcism could also be said about exorcisms that are performed by heathen priests or spiritistic mediums or magicians whether they be Jews or Gentiles. Jesus seems to imply in his remarks to His enemies in Matthew 12 that Jewish exorcists were able to cast out demons. Are we to assume that these men were servants of God who used the power of His Word to control evil spirits? Josephus says that they used incantations invented by Solomon, which we can hardly understand to be part of God's revelation. If the devil can through such apparent miracles attract men away from God's revelation, it would only be another way of manifesting his diabolical cleverness, about which the Bible leaves us in no doubt.

Some of the devilish cleverness with which the devil operates is seen in the biblical accounts of exorcism. A number of times the record refers to the fact that the devils confessed that Jesus was the Messiah and the Son of God (Luke 4:34,41; 8:28). The people recognized that these were demons speaking. For such a demon to speak so highly of Jesus is a clever attempt at discrediting the Savior, and it may be that the charge of the Pharisees that Jesus Himself was in league with the devil may have stemmed originally from some of the suggestions made by the devil in this way.

On the other hand, we also know that Catholic exorcists together with the names of the saints also use the name of Jesus; and side by side with their prayers to Mary, they also address prayers to the Triune God. We know that the Word of God is effective even when used by wicked men. The name of Jesus and the biblical doctrine, which is stressed in the Ritual of Exorcism, that Christ has come to destroy the power of the devil and has actually destroyed it by His death and resurrection are surely terrifying to the devil even when they are proclaimed by men who deny other basic truths of Christianity. Could they therefore be exorcisms in Jesus' name? Luther did not believe this was the case. In his *Tischreden* he is quoted as saying that the Roman exorcists were charmers or sorcerers and that the devil left the possessed when exorcised by them in order to bring the people into greater bondage.[11]

All of this illustrates once more how careful we must be in evaluating the occult and in making statements concerning the subject.

CAN MIRACLES EVER BE DONE IN SUPPORT OF FALSE DOCTRINE?

It is sometimes asked whether it is correct to say that God will

117

never permit any miracle to be performed to support false doctrine. If we mean by "miracle" any supernatural event that defies explanation on the basis of purely natural causes, without reference to the power behind the "miracle," I would doubt very much whether such an axiom can be supported by Scripture. Can we say beyond question that the "miracles" of the magicians of Pharaoh were nothing but trickery? Or is it possible that we are here dealing with spiritistic apports? When Moses in Deuteronomy 13 spoke of signs and wonders performed by false prophets, must we assume that these miracles are pure fraud and that nothing supernatural is involved? And we might ask again, when Paul spoke of the miracles, the signs and the lying wonders of Antichrist, must we assume that these, too, are the products of pure deception and involve nothing more than the lies with which the servants of Satan deceive those whom they seek to win to their false doctrine?

Such questions are also very relevant when we deal with the charismatic movement. Can we really say beyond question, as we are often tempted to say, that tongues and healings are always nothing more than autosuggestion? Can we really say beyond question that the Holy Ghost never gives men the gift of tongues or of healing today? Or can we say without question, the way we say that Jesus is our Savior, that the devil could not mimic the Pentecostal miracles of the early church?

Thank God, we do not need to answer those questions. "The secret things belong to the Lord our God; but those things which are revealed belong unto us and to our children forever." What this means, of course, is that the revelation of God, as we have it in the Scriptures, must be and remain the only norm by which all occult or supernatural events must be judged. Instead of saying that God would never permit a miracle to be performed by a false teacher in support of false doctrine, we ought to say that any miracle, real or imagined, that is performed in support of false doctrine is not from God. In other words, it is not a divine miracle but Satanic witchcraft. When we are told, for example, that the world's leading spokesman for Pentecostalism, David du Plessis, teaches that Luther was wrong and the Roman Catholic Church right on the doctrine of justification,[12] we ought no longer to be surprised if the miracles and signs and lying wonders that support Antichrist are also found in Pentecostalism. For such remarks can only serve to

118

promote the first great lie of Satan, namely, that men can find salvation only through what they do for themselves rather than in what God has done and still does for them.

CAN A CHRISTIAN BE POSSESSED

Another subject that is often debated is the question of whether the devil is able to possess the body and mind of a Christian. Our dogmaticians make a sharp distinction between "bodily possession" and "spiritual possession." Some modern writers make a similar distinction when they speak of demonic obsession and demonic possession.

While the dogmaticians are agreed that spiritual possession is impossible in the case of a Christian, they are not unanimous in the opinion that a Christian cannot be possessed in a bodily way. Andreas Quenstedt, who is one of the greatest dogmaticians of the Lutheran Church, says that the subject of possession is not only the unbeliever but also occasionally a pious man, and that in His secret counsel God sometimes permits also upright men to become possessed.[13] Adolf Hoenecke, on the other hand, in his *Dogmatik* seems to deny this possibility.[14] Franz Pieper, however, agrees with Quenstedt and says, "Also children of God may suffer this affliction."[15] As evidence he cites the Gadarene demoniac. The biblical account, however, allows us to look upon the conversion of this demoniac as taking place after his deliverance. Quenstedt cites the case of the possessed child, of whose faith, however, the Bible says nothing at all. Dr. Walther, in his *Pastorale*, quotes, apparently with approval, the advice that in free moments the possessed may be given the Lord's Supper and that the possessed should be assured that they are not accountable for the blasphemies uttered in the paroxyms of possession.[16]

My own personal opinion is that we can not answer this question dogmatically. The only biblical account which, in my judgment, would come close to giving an answer is that of the woman in Luke 13, who had a "spirit of weakness" of whom Jesus says that Satan had bound her for eighteen years. The expression "to have a spirit" is used of a clear case of possession earlier in Luke's Gospel (4:33), but there the spirit is defined as "the spirit of an unclean demon." The deaf and dumb spirit spoken of by Mark (9:17) is also later called an "unclean" spirit. The description of the woman in Luke 13, does not enable us to say beyond question that she was demonized, although Jesus' remark that she was a daughter of Abraham indicates that she was a believing child of God. While the matter therefore must remain an open question in dogmatics, I would be inclined to agree with Dr. Walther that we can assume that also believers can be possessed, but that they should be comforted with the assurance that the Lord Jesus has taken away their sins and will not hold them accountable for obscenities and blasphemies which they have uttered involuntarily. On the other hand, they should be reminded of the promise of God that says, "Resist the devil and he will flee from you."

THE DEFEAT OF THE DEVIL BY CHRIST

We can be certain that in dealing with the occult, properly defined, we are dealing with the lies of Satan. If no direct spirit agency is involved and the claim to supernatural knowledge or power is a fraud, the purposes of the devil are still being served. The astrologer who operates with clever psychological tricks and whose pronouncements are pure deception is still doing the devil's work in directing the attention of men away from God's grace to material wealth and success as the source of happiness.

When, however, remarkable and unexplainable results are achieved through the various forms of divination, magic, witchcraft, and spiritism, we may with justification suspect that we are dealing with the intrusion of evil spirits into our material world. Believing Christians ought not to welcome with open arms the efforts of men to demonstrate the fraudulence of the occult, if those efforts proceed from the premise that only that which is natural can truly exist. By the same token they ought to recognize the danger of dealing even in play or for curiosity's sake with the occult.

In fact, we may view all practitioners of the occult as being to some extent possessed by the devil, either consciously or unconsciously, either voluntarily or in an involuntary way. The spiritist medium who calls upon the spirits of the dead is actually inviting demons to come and speak through her. The practitioner of astral projection who visits places far away and can report in detail what he has seen is opening his mind to demonic forces which may eventually take over complete control. One of the demoniacs whose case is reported in *Hostage to the Devil* after his recovery said,

Of myself, I could not see things happening hundreds of miles away, read the future, see the past, peer with minute detail into people's minds. I could give the illusion of these only by being prompted by someone who could see from a great distance, could read the future, had a detailed knowledge of the past, could peer into people's minds.[17]

But above all else, in all our dealings with the occult we ought to keep in view the teaching of Scripture that Satan has been defeated by the Son of God who was manifested to destroy the works of the devil and that we, too, are enabled by Christ to defeat him with the blood of the Lamb and the Gospel we proclaim. If our study of the occult has prompted us to look more consistently to Christ as the source of our strength and to pray more devoutly "Let Thy holy angel be with me that the wicked foe may have no power over me," it will not have been a waste of time.

SOURCES

Chapter V

1. Baroja, op. cit., pp. 229f; 256f.
2. Petersen, *Those Curious New Cults*, p. 92.
3. Ibid., p. 93.
4. Gary Wilburn, *The Fortune Sellers*, Glendale, Calif,. G/L Publications, 1972, p. 146.
5. Tiryakian, op. cit., p. 224f.
6. *Those Curious New Cults*, p. 98.
7. Mike Warnke, *The Satan Seller*, Plainfield, New Jersey, Logos International, 1972.
8. Puharich, op. cit., p. 254.
9. "The False Angel of Light," *Christianity Today*, XX, 19 (June 18, 1976), p. 22.
10. Cp. Mk 3:26 ("if Satan rise up against himself"); Lk 11:8 ("if Satan also be divided against himself").
11. Quoted by Walther, *Pastoraltheologie*, St. Louis, Concordia, 1906, pp. 294f.
12. *Christian News*, 9, 42 (10/25/76), p. 3.
13. *Middler Dogmatics Notes*, Wisconsin Lutheran Seminary, p. 90.
14. Adolf Hoenecke, *Evangelische-Lutherische Dogmatik*, Milwaukee, Northwestern Publishing House, 1909, II, 296.
15. Francis Pieper, *Christian Dogmatics*, St. Louis, Concordia, 1950, I, 509.
16. Walther, op. cit., p. 295.
17. Martin, op. cit. p. 403f.

SCRIPTURAL INDEX

Scripture	Page	Scripture	Page
Gn 1:14	16	2 Kg 17:17	53
Gn 1:31	103	Is 1:1	21
Gn 3:1-5	4,104,116	Is 8:19,20	53,59
Gn 3:15	105	Is 14:12	105
Gn 4:1	39	Is 34:16	6
Gn 18:2	70	Is 41:22,23	6
Gn 20:3	20	Is 44:6-8	6
Gn 30:37	38,39	Is 44:25	24
Gn 31:10-12	40	Is 47:13,14	1,11
Gn 31:11	20	Jr 23:27	21
Gn 31:24	20	Ez 21:21	17
Gn 32:10	39	Dn 2:1-49	20,53
Gn 37:5-11	20	Dn 2:28	3
Gn 40:5-23	20	Dn 7:1	20
Gn 41:1-36	20	Nah 3:4	53
Gn 41:8	33	Mt 2:1	8
Gn 41:16	3	Mt 2:12	20
Ex 3&4	32	Mt 2:13	20
Ex 3:12	67	Mt 4:3	105
Ex 4:8,9	32	Mt 4:8,9	103,106
Ex 4:30,31	32	Mt 4:24	79
Ex 7:1	2	Mt 8:16	30
Ex 7:11	31,35,72,118	Mt 9:23	30
Ex 8:18,19	1,32,53	Mt 9:32	80
Ex 9:11	53	Mt 12:22	80
Ex 22:18	35,53	Mt 12:26	115
Lv 16:8	105	Mt 12:27	117
Lv 19:26	24	Mt 13:9	105
Nu 12:6	20	Mt 15:21	80
Dt 13	7,33,35,118	Mt 17:14	80
Dt 18:10-12	17,24,28,59	Mk 1:23	80
Dt 18:22	7,24,58	Mk 5:9	89,119
Dt 29:29	114,115,118	Mk 5:34	91
1 Sm 6:14	81	Mk 5:38	30
1 Sm 9:1-20	1	Mk 7:24	80
1 Sm 9:20	3	Mk 9:1	7
1 Sm 15:19,28	58	Mk 9:17,18	80,91,119
1 Sm 28:1-25	56-58	Lk 1:11-37	4
1 Sm 28:19	5	Lk 4:5-7	106
1 Kg 3:5	20	Lk 4:33	80,119
1 Kg 18:12	72	Lk 4:34,41	117
1 Kg 22:1-38	2,24	Lk 7:11	30
1 Kg 22:22	6	Lk 8:2	78
2 Kg 1:2	105	Lk 8:28	117
2 Kg 2:11	70	Lk 8:30	89
2 Kg 6:17	70	Lk 8:49	30
2 Kg 7:1	3	Lk 9:38	80

Scripture	Page	Scripture	Page
Lk 11:14	80	2 Cor 4:4	105
Lk 11:21,22	78	2 Cor 5:4	113
Lk 13:11	79,119,120	2 Cor 12:1-4	47
Lk 13:16	80	Ga 5:20	53
Lk 22:50	30	Eph 2:2	105
Jn 3:2	29,33	Col 1:16	103
Jn 3:7	74	2 Th 2:9	116
Jn 8:44	104	1 Tm 4:1	6,112
Jn 8:59	72	2 Tm 2:26	113
Jn 9:1-7	30,39	He 1:1-3	29
Jn 10:22-38	29	Ja 4:7	97,120
Jn 10:25,38	33	1 Pe 5:8	104,105
Jn 11:43	30	2 Pe 2:4	103
Jn 12:31	105,116	1 Jn 3:8	105
Jn 12:37	33	1 Jn 4:1	6
Jn 20:30,31	29,33	Jd 6	103
Ac 8:9-24	53	Re 1:1	3,4
Ac 8:18	42	Re 9:11	104
Ac 8:39	72	Re 12:7-11	105
Ac 13:6-11	53	Re 12:9	104
Ac 16:16	81	Re 12:11	103
Ac 16:19	82	Re 17:1	4
Ac 19:13-16	86	Re 20:10	105
Ac 19:19	53	Re 21:8	53
Ro 16:25	114	Re 21:9	4
1 Cor 8:4	112	Re 22:8	4
1 Cor 10:20	67,103,105,112	Re 22:15	53